YOUR
SIGNATURE
PATH

Photo: Sheila Kelly

YOUR SIGNATURE PATH

Gaining
New
Perspectives
on
Life
and
Work

GEOFFREY M. BELLMAN

Berrett-Koehler Publishers
San Francisco

Berrett-Koehler Publishers, Inc.
450 Sansome Street, Suite 1200
San Francisco, CA 94111-3320
Tel: (415) 288-0260   Fax: (415) 362-2512

Ordering Information

Individual sales. Berrett-Koehler publications are available through most bookstores. They can also be ordered direct from Berrett-Koehler at the address above.

Quantity sales. Special discounts are available on quantity purchases by corporations, associations, and others. For details, contact the "Special Sales Department" at the Berrett-Koehler address above.

Orders for college textbook/course adoption use. Please contact Berrett-Koehler Publishers at the address above.

Orders by U.S. trade bookstores and wholesalers. Please contact Publishers Group West, 4065 Hollis Street, Box 8843, Emeryville, CA 94662. Tel: (510) 658-3453; 1-800-788-3123. Fax: (510) 658-1834

Printed in the United States of America

 Printed on acid-free and recycled paper that is composed of 50% recovered fiber, including 10% postconsumer waste.

Library of Congress Cataloging-in-Publication Data
Bellman, Geoffrey M., 1938–
        Your signature path / Geoffrey Bellman. — 1st ed.
              p. cm.
        Includes index.
        ISBN 1-57675-004-3 (alk. paper)
            1. Life. 2. Self-realization. 3. Self (Philosphy) I. Title.
        BD431.B386   1996
        170'.44--dc20   96-31515
                                                     CIP

First Edition
99   98   97   96   10   9   8   7   6   5   4   3   2   1

A Bard Books, Inc., Production
Production manager: Sherry Sprague
Copyediting and proofreading: Helen Hyams
Indexing: Linda Webster
Interior design and composition: Joel Friedlander Publishing Services
Cover: Cassandra Chu

For Sheila Kelly
on our thirty-second anniversary

Contents

Preface

We come into the world without intending to.
We will likely leave in the same way.
In between, we live, love, and work.
We make the difference we will make.

THIS BOOK HELPS YOU TO EXPLORE the difference you intend to make in between. It is about the path you create with your wondering and wandering, searching and finding. It is about your single path with its twists and turns, now looking down from a peak, now alone in the desert. This path began with your birth and ends when your life ends. You are on that path now and everything, everyone, you touch continues it. No one ever has or ever will take this path again. It is your signature across the surface of the earth.

Step back from your path and you can see the paths of people around you, each one as unique as yours in its direction and movement. Signature upon signature as these many paths meet, cross over each other, join, create patterns, align, and separate. They are the evidence of our combined experience playing out on the face of the earth.

This book assumes that you want to be thoughtful and intentional about what you are doing on your path. You may have grand or small ambitions, but you want to live with integrity and you want to grow in the process of living. You want to become yourself more fully while contributing to the world. Reading this book could be part of your continuing transformation of yourself. This book strengthens your ability to see your path. It is more about seeing, and acting on what you see, than it is about gaining brand-new skills. It helps you to use your present skills better by altering how you see the world around you. When you change how you see, that new seeing changes how you act. The book asks you to look through different lenses from those you might ordinarily use.

Your Signature Path is my best statement so far about combining good work with good love in a meaningful life. The book will frequently discuss work and love; it will link them and marry them for life, as I believe they ought to be married. Work and love are essential to life and are often unnaturally separated in the workplace; in this book I attempt to rejoin them. My experience as a management consultant reinforces my belief in work as a path to our individual greatness. I suspect that this fits with your aspirations, too.

This is a book for people who:

o Live and work, and find the two inseparable

o Are caught up in the whirl of life, love, and work

o Find it difficult to balance their lives

o Are intent on learning more of what life is about

o Want to know that they are not alone in these pursuits

o Want the stimulation of other people's ideas

In short, it is for reflective, invested people who care about the difference they are making in the world.

The book grew out of my notes to myself. It began not as an outline with structure and purpose, but as an electronic journal of my own fleeting and occasionally shadowy thoughts about what was happening in my life. After I had 250 pages of notes in my computer, I printed them out and read what I had been thinking about. What you are reading grew out of that pile of pages, and I grew with it. The book is best read a chapter or two at a time, with frequent breaks to reflect. You do not need to read all of it to appreciate it; many chapters stand well on their own. I offer this book as a guide on your signature path.

Geoffrey M. Bellman
Seattle, Washington
July 1996

Acknowledgments

IF YOU HAVE NOT YET WRITTEN A BOOK, you may not realize how much support is needed to bring an author from concept to reality. That support was especially important to this book. This is my fourth book with Ray Bard at Bard Books. We have grown in our appreciation of each other while producing these books. This is my third book published by Steven Piersanti, the second with him at his own publishing firm, Berrett-Koehler. The world needs more publishers like Berrett-Koehler. The staff is a delight to work with; they treat their writers and readers with respect and love.

Special thanks to my content editor, Patricia Galagan, who was enormously helpful in pulling this manuscript together. And thanks to the readers of the third-draft manuscript: Roy Doughty, Alan Green, Sheila Kelly, Jennifer Myers, Jan Nickerson, and Paul Wright. I am sure all of you will recognize the difference made by your collective efforts. Frank Basler, Jeananne Oliphant, and Leslie Stephen read a first draft and encouraged me with suggestions that helped shape the book. Forrest Belcher offered perspective along the way. Betsy McCarthy typed into the night ensuring that deadlines would be met. My wife, Sheila Kelly, helped in each step of the book's development, from concept to final draft. Without her, this book simply would not have been created. And last of all, thank you to my friends and clients from whom I have learned so much on my own signature path.

What Is The Meaning of Your Life

The world is a dream within a dream;
As we grow older, each step is an awakening.

—SIR WALTER SCOTT

BILLIONS OF PEOPLE HAVE WALKED THE EARTH. Over five billion of us are here right now. We each move through our lives, finding our way, cutting our paths through the world. As we make these paths, we create our unique selves. Follow any one of us for a day, a week, and you will see us define ourselves by how we move along our unique paths. Thousands of people have walked this same ground before us, but we each walk it in our own way. Map our individual paths across the surface of this planet and see the peaks we have attained, the circles in which we have turned, and the well-worn routes we have favored. These are our signature paths.

A view through a telescope from the moon would show us as billions of tiny dots, each moving, converging, diverging, and scattering in many directions. The movement would provoke curiosity. Why are those particular dots converging on one dot? Why are those others running together? Why did these four split off from fifty others? Some dots seem to be creating communities. Others appear to be defining themselves as separate. The patterns that are created suggest meaning, but what is it? The meaning behind the movement does not reveal itself. Why is she going to a library? Why do they leave home at the same time each day?

Why is he taking a bus across town to see her? Why are those children sitting in rows at computers? "Why?" is the unanswered question in the view through the telescope. To answer the question, we must look into each dot, each person.

Our beginnings and endings have an apparent randomness. Our dot appears and begins to move on its path from its first breath. Many years later, the path stops; our dot disappears. We die in the middle of our sleep, or dinner, or a thought, on the way to something else. From this perspective, our dots are less notable for their accomplishments than for their movement. It is this movement that we will concentrate on in this book.

Each person's path across the face of the earth moves toward his or her unique purpose; watch and you will see the search for purpose in this movement. Look at my path to this point in my life and you will see the actions that led me to this keyboard rapping out this page, and a look back down your life path would show what brought you to this page. We each arrive at this moment with purpose. Many intentions and questions brought us here: What is the meaning of my life? Why do I keep doing this work? How do I regain life balance? What will I do next? What is becoming of me? What can I do about it? These questions are filled with purpose and this book is filled with these questions. The book encourages and guides you in finding your answers; it does this through the metaphor of the path: you on your path through the world.

The book is organized around three essential elements of your signature path: your self, your world, and your path:

o *Your self* includes your body, mind, and heart, absorbing the world and making some sense out of it. This is your very public self, visible, tangible, active; it is also your private self, which you may reveal or conceal, the self that immediately directs much of what you do. And beyond that, it is your reflective self, which is standing back processing, intuiting, learning, and creating sense from all the experience. This self relates one moment to the next, and to ten years ago and five years from now. This is your aspiring, valuing self that chooses and makes paths.

○ *Your world* is the external world that you encounter through your senses. You move through this world, you adapt to it, and, in small ways, it adapts to you as you move across its surface. It consists of everything outside of you—people, places, things, nouns. It is all the "stuff" out there that can be appreciated, moved, acquired, consumed, destroyed, valued, loved, hated, or polished.

○ *Your path* is where you touch the world. It is the difference you make by being there. It is made up of the trail of footprints, lip prints, handprints, even the fingerprints you are leaving on this page. It is every point at which you make physical contact with the world.

Look back over your shoulder. This is your path—leading from where you came from to where you are. Your path includes all that you have done that you cannot change, right up to this moment. Your future path comes into existence through what you are doing in the present. The present is that small part of the path that you can do something about.

EXERCISE

Contact

1. Notice where you are right now. Notice where gravity is helping you to make physical contact with the world. Notice where you touch this book, how you are supporting the book. Notice what supports you as you support the book. And notice what supports whatever is supporting you. Imagine the foundation of connections that exist between the book and the earth. For example, book, hand, body, chair, carpet, floor, foundation, and earth. Imagine all that is physically involved in connecting you to the earth. Once you have done that, move on.

2. Think about where you have been during the last two days as if you were filming yourself. Follow your path of prints back through the last two days. Recall what you touched, who you touched, where you walked, sat, slept, where you physically were.

3. Next, imagine where you will be going tomorrow. Picture the path you anticipate to be ahead of you. Picture yourself get-

ting up and moving through the day. If it were on film, what would you see? When you have done that, return to read the next paragraph.

This short pause on your path is to help you experience the ideas of self, world, and path in a more physical way, which is perhaps a less familiar perspective for you. As this book's subtitle says, we are gaining new perspectives on life and work. This was just the first of many times this book will ask you to try on a different view of the world. These exercises are intended to draw you into the content of the book. Your life and work experience will be woven into these pages. It would be lopsided without your ideas and feelings, opinions and insights. The book needs your engagement with it to work; the exercises provide that active engagement. Here's the deal: I will offer thoughts and exercises to engage you more deeply in thinking about your life. Your side of this deal is to be open to these thoughts and experiences. How does that sound? I'll proceed with that in mind. And you, of course, will do as you choose.

Early on in this book, you will find that you need paper and pen. Or a legal pad, or a laptop, or a journal, or one of those blank books that are available at your bookstore. While you are reading, you will have nearly forty opportunities to pause, think, and write. It might be nice to have all that thinking and writing collected in one place; that's why I suggest a journal. The book's margins or scraps of paper can work too, but a journal is better. Write regularly while you are reading. Capture thoughts, feelings, and perspectives. And keep all of the notes you take while reading this book; you will be referring back to them. Your notes document your conversations with yourself. Some of you are used to writing and already keep notes about your life. Others of you are lucky to have time to read a book, much less write about what you read! It is enough to just read this book, but keeping notes will create a larger learning experience for you.

In the beginning this book was a collection of thoughts for myself. It has turned outward and evolved into a book with you, the reader, in mind. A role has emerged for me in this book. I now see myself as a guide, similar to the guides you might have for an outdoor wilderness experience, though this is an indoor wilderness experience! I am here to help you make your paths through new territory. As your guide, I will help you to pay attention to what surrounds you in life and work. I hope to help you see and interpret your surroundings differently. I do not know where you are going on this path you are making; you have to decide that for yourself. But I do know about path making and the wilderness through which you are cutting your path. This is familiar country for me and I will help you with your explorations. I live in this indoor wilderness, I love it, and I love helping you learn about it. Let's move into Part One, "Your Self."

Your
Self

*All the greatest and most important problems of life are
fundamentally insoluble. . . . They can never be solved, but
only outgrown. This "outgrowing" proved [to] require a new
level of consciousness. Some higher or wider interest
appeared on the . . . horizon, and through this broadening of
. . . outlook, the insoluble problem lost its urgency. It was not
solved logically in its own terms but faded when confronted
with a new and stronger image.*

—CARL JUNG

FROM THE BEGINNING TO THE END of this book, we are going to
be looking at our selves, our world, and our paths from new perspectives. Together, we will attempt to create the new "consciousness" that Carl Jung wrote about. In a few pages, you will
step into thoughts and experiences intended to give you "new
and stronger images" of yourself. You will be seeing yourself from
angles and altitudes other than those in which you habitually
exist. By mentioning this early, I intend to prepare you for the
exercises offered to you in this book, but I especially want to
ready you for the exercises in Part One, which is centered on your
self. This is the "toe-in-the-water" of what I hope will be a nice,
warm bath.

Imagine going outside, finding a bare square foot of brown
dirt, and smoothing its surface with the side of your hand. Imagine using your finger to sign your name in the soil. Imagine that.
Or do it. When you touch the soil and furrow it with your finger,
you demonstrate in a small way what *Your Signature Path* is all
about. Your unique, hard-to-duplicate signature is on this small
piece of earth. You created this small difference in your unique
way. And that difference parallels the much larger writing you are

doing on the earth in your constant contact with it. Imagine the furrows you create there! Imagine the trails you take, the routes you repeat, the people and places and things you touch along the way. All of that is part of your signature path on this planet.

Just as you wrote your name in the dirt in your own special way, so you will mark the earth in your own unique way. Part One is designed to help you reflect upon and anticipate the steps you take along your path.

Some last suggestions before you jump in:

o Expect to do something as a result of reading this book, and to do it now, not later.

o Notice your internal reactions to what you read. See discomfort not as something to be avoided but as a learning possibility. Move toward it, rather than away from it.

o Enjoy this book! For some people it is just delicious! Others find that it is not to their taste. Consume it as you might the offerings of another culture's kitchen.

And here come the appetizers!

CHAPTER ONE

Sight Building

MUCH OF THE FIRST QUARTER OF OUR LIVES is given to others' building of knowledge and skills in us. Along with all that useful (and not too useful) learning, we are also acquiring a major implied tenet of our formal education: people learn through being taught. Provide people with new knowledge and teach them new skills; this is the way to change them. But this is not the only way we learn, it is not the primary way we learn, and it is not even the best way to learn much of the time, especially for adults.

An alternative to knowledge and skill building is sight building—seeing the world in new ways and behaving with this new perception in mind. When we see the world differently, we have to honor this new perspective. Our actions will be altered by what we now see; we will use our old skills in new ways. Our new perspective may be as small as discovering a "happy and motivated" co-worker in tears and finding that it affects all of our subsequent actions with that person. Or it may be as large as a new appreciation of our own mortality, as often happens at the death of a parent. The world is not the same and our own lives are not the same; our behavior can change from that moment on.

The accumulated experience of getting through life is accompanied by a reliance on the abilities that we think got us here. We say, "I tried it, it worked, I'll try it again." We often use these abilities to the point of entrenching ourselves in their familiar routines. Repeating what has worked has not only gotten us where we are; it also makes it more difficult to do something else. We say, "I've always done it this way, it's working, why switch?" Long, successful life experience can block receptiveness to new perspectives and new learning. Long, unsuccessful experience can do the same. We say, "I've always done it this way, I'm suspicious of other ways. So it's not working; I'm too old to learn." Repetition of a skill, a process, or an experience reinforces it. Every time we do it, we are quietly saying, "This is the best way to do it." My path becomes my rut becomes my trench.

Enter perspective: you fall in love, a child is born, a spouse leaves, a lottery ticket wins, a friend gets cancer. In a moment, your life changes. It looks different than it did a few days ago. Your life will never be the same; you will never be the same. Your behavior changes and you adapt to the way you see things now.

What do all of these life-altering experiences have in common? They affect the way we see the world. It really does look different to us. What we place in the foreground is different. Take having your first baby or having your first grandchild. Living in the world is a new experience, whether the baby is with you or not. You will see babies that you didn't see before. Babies have always been there but were less important to you. You will likely start talking to babies, showing pictures of babies, worrying about babies you see in the evening news. I have heard a number of executives say that they started looking at their company differently when they began thinking about the world they are going to leave for their grandchildren. Perspective becomes action.

When that new perspective takes over, it inherits the same old skills that were there with the old perspective. But the new view of the world can use those old skills to new purpose. We don't always need new skills to be successful; we often just need a new perspective. We need to put on new glasses, though it is not that easy. We actually have more choice about the skills we use than about the perspectives we take on. Skills are tools we can pick up or put down. Perspectives are ways of seeing that become part of us. Once they have been incorporated, they cannot easily be set aside.

Another View

We can be intentional about gaining perspective; we don't have to just sit around and wait for it. Here are some ways to set about seeing the world in other ways, at least temporarily. Which one of these would you like to do? Pick one and do it!

EXERCISE

- ○ Spend an afternoon with someone under ten. Try to see the world from the child's view. Afterward, explain the difference between your view and the child's to someone.

- ○ Ask someone to describe what is going on in his or her life now. Express back what you heard and felt as you listened.

- ○ Explain an old problem in a new way—for example, by describing the advantages of having the problem, rather than its disadvantages.

- ○ Write a long letter to either or both of your parents telling them what they gave you that helps you to succeed with your life. After writing the letter, decide whether you want to send it.

- ○ Summon up all of your optimism for this planet and write a statement about your hopes for its future. If you already live in a perspective of optimism, bring forth all your concerns and write about them.

- ○ If you knew you were going to die in six months, what would you do in the interim? Think about it and write about it.

- ○ Bring together people who are invested in an issue, especially people you do not ordinarily work with. Spend your time asking questions of them, listening, and noting their answers. Now read your notes; what did you learn?

o Write a "love letter" to someone you have not expressed your feelings to in a long time. Note how your feelings have developed.

o Volunteer at a homeless shelter or hospice. Reflect on residing in such a place.

o Talk with someone of a different race, religion, or gender about how the two of you differ. Consider how those differences affect your relationship.

Do at least one of these. If you gain some new perspective from it, do another, and if you gain *no* new perspective, try another. Whatever you choose, make notes on what you see differently as a result. Writing about it will help you to incorporate it into your perspectives on the world.

Jumping into these short exercises moves you physically and mentally to a place you might not ordinarily be. When you see differently, you respond differently. Most learning comes from your engagement with the world around you, what you absorb, and what you do with what you retain. These exercises encourage you to seek out and try on alternative realities. Experiencing them could bring surprise or shock, delight or depression. Whatever you learn will become part of you.

CHAPTER TWO

Reaching for Your Fulfillment

YOUR PATH BEGAN AT YOUR BIRTH. You probably have some sense of where you are on that path right now and its direction and slope. You are going somewhere. Where you are going may not be very clear, but you are intentional about it. Implied purpose supports your movement on your path.

One of the primary ways many of us seek our purpose is through our work. In that job, through these roles, we attempt to serve customers, satisfy employers, get along with co-workers, earn a living, and give some small expression to the person within who cries out to experience life. We give most of our waking hours to this work, and most of our life energy. You pick the next line:

"There *must* be some purpose in this besides meeting everyone else's needs!"

"*Can't* there be some purpose in this beyond the money?"

"There *is* a larger purpose to this!"

This chapter is about your reach for purpose and fulfillment, especially through the work you do.

Think of people you know who are keenly interested in what they are doing, particularly those who are pursuing something of their own free will. Why is she so joyful in this line of work? Why does he pursue this hobby? Why do you become so fascinated with some parts of your life? In some ways, she, he, and you are incomplete and your focus or fascination has to do with reaching for your potential. Whether the fascination is fly fishing or furniture, gardening or gigabytes, animals or analysis, most of us are trying to express and complete ourselves. As much as we already know, we still want to learn more, to become more.

Hows and Whys

What are you invested in? What do you willingly return to on a regular basis, especially in your work? Some of you may be saying, "Are you *kidding?* Through my *work?*" Yes, let's start there because it relates to your purpose.

This exercise has great potential, depending on what you choose to do with it. It works well if you go through it with another person. It works fine if you take ten minutes to do it alone or spend hours on it. I'll describe it from the doing-it-alone perspective, because you are the only one I know for sure is here:

1. Get two sheets of paper, or open to two facing pages in your journal. With lines, divide each of these two pages into four horizontal rows. These horizontal rows are to limit the amount of work you do as you think through the coming steps.

2. Next, ask this question of yourself: "What do I do at work?" Briefly note your answer in the top row on the left page. Do that now in one sentence or so. Do it quickly, without a lot of thought.

3. Ask yourself, "How do I do that?" Briefly note your answer in the second row on the left page. Write just a sentence or two.

4. Now ask yourself, "And how do I do that?" Again, briefly note your answer in the third row.

5. Finally, ask yourself, "And how do I do that?" Write this last response in the last row of the left page. This last How may be difficult, but try it.

6. The left page now contains a short description of what you do, followed by your three How responses. Before you move on, read it over and look for patterns in what you have written. Notice any feelings this short writing experience generated. Consider the direction in which these How questions took you. Consider when and how often you talk with others about how you do your work. Make a few notes on the thoughts and feelings this page generated. Then go on to the next page.

7. Read aloud your answer to the "What do I do at work?" question from the first row of the left page.

8. Turning to the right page, ask yourself, "Why is that important to me?" Note your brief response in the top row of this page. Do this quickly. Notice the feelings it evokes.

9. Now ask yourself again, "Why is that important to me?" Note your response in the second row.

10. Then ask yourself, "And why is that important to me?" Write down your response in the third row. Pause to notice your feelings as you do this.

11. One last time, ask yourself, "And why is that important to me?" Write it down. This is the fourth and last time.

12. What generally did you write about on the second page? Do you see any patterns? How easy or difficult was this to do? What were the strongest feelings you had while doing this? What is the apparent destination of this chain of responses? How often do you talk with others about the kinds of things you just wrote? Respond to each of these questions, making

a few notes to yourself, or talk with someone about your responses.

13. Now try a comparison. How did all that you wrote, thought, and felt for the Why questions compare to your responses to the How questions? Really think about this, come up with some answers, and make a few last notes.

Now let's talk about the exercise. Most people working through these Hows and Whys find that their two pages head off in quite different directions. The Hows tend toward the methodologies, the practices, the tasks involved in getting work done. The Whys more often lead to the reasons for work, its deeper meaning, the aspirations that lie behind it—toward the real purposes of their lives. Most people find the Hows easier to think about and talk about with others; the Whys seem to lead in a more personal direction. People are often uneasy about sharing their Whys with others. They may feel invaded when asked about them, believing that they are private. The Hows tend to take us deeper into the past; the Whys move us toward the future.

At work, we spend lots of time on the Hows. When we gather with others who do the same kind of work, the Hows seem to predominate. They are the way we get things done. Being practical people, we often meet with others to get things done. In the process, we get so caught up in the Hows that we lose the reasons why we are doing what we are doing and feel "Ours is not to reason why . . ." Our focus on practice can lead us away from our purpose. Our methods can lead us away from our meaning.

My friend Lucy passed through town recently, stopping to visit with me between her connecting flights. In our two hours together at the airport, I heard about four months of her life: two months back and two months projected into the future. Lucy does an excellent job of organizing her life around her work and the travel it requires. She knows where she has been or will be every waking moment, and she takes some pride in this. But the questions that occupied the second hour of our time together were Whys. To paraphrase Lucy, "I know how to do the work very well. I know how to organize my time and travel to get the maximum accomplished. But lately, while flying along at thirty-five thousand feet, I've been asking myself, why am I on this plane? Where am I going? I know my work destination, but what's my life destination? I'm all scheduled up and wonder where I'm going!" She recognizes the widening gap between her practice and her purpose, her methods and her meaning.

Whys lift us toward our aspirations. In the Whys lies the possibility of discovering a higher purpose. Our Whys are more separate and personal, often remaining unexpressed behind our actions. Hows carry us into the details of getting the work done. We share them with others as a part of the work. The Hows without the Whys lead to action without reason or meaning. Whys without Hows lead to unrooted, unrealistic, unacted-upon ideas.

People have been intrigued with the "Hows and Whys" exercise. Through it, we recount what we do, how we do it, our reasons for doing it, and our reasons for working. All of this leads toward reasons for being. The Whys speak to our motivation, our essence, our passion. Here are some practical uses of this exploration:

o Try the experience with someone close to you and see what you learn about each other. Compare notes; talk. Find out what your Hows and Whys have to do with your friendship.

o Carry your "Hows and Whys" pages with you for a week. Make a point of reading them at least once a day. Notice what impact this has on your perspective and action, if any.

o Complete the exercise again, this time asking yourself, "What do I do at play?" Compare your responses to the work responses.

Everyone you know has Whys, whether they have explored them or not, and their reasons for doing what they are doing at work, at home, or in meetings are related to these Whys. If you hope to influence the people around you—those co-workers, these kids, this spouse, these parents, that friend—then appeal to their Whys.

Young children frequently ask "Why?" "Why?" and "Why?" They are on a search for the meaning of all that surrounds them, a search that deserves encouragement. How do you support their inquiries?

Recall revolutions—political revolutions, industrial revolutions, social revolutions. What united the people that made those revolutions happen? Whys. The slogans, the speeches, the songs are filled with Whys. They appeal to our deep meaning and life purpose. These Whys unite people in common cause. We often need small revolutions in work groups, communities, families, or ourselves, revolutions that come through discovering the power of shared Whys.

Our organizations—home, work, and community—do a good job of helping us to think about the Hows. Each of us has to take responsibility for thinking about our Whys. If we don't think about them, others will. They will assign meanings to our work and lives that may not fit with the meanings we would assign. Because our Whys have to do with our motivation, our purpose, and our principles, we must figure them out for ourselves.

We can slip into thoughtless patterns that become ruts. These patterns involve movement, but without reflection on our movement's impact on the world, they are just the opposite of what our signature path is about. Or we become what others want—our boss, our spouse, our neighbors, our children, our government, our club. We "decide" that what they think is best, putting aside what we want, making them responsible for us. We say, "I couldn't help it . . ." "She made me do it . . ." "If I hadn't, he would have gotten mad . . ." "We know what they want and we'd better give it to them." How often do our reasons contain the names of others? How often do we make others responsible for our actions?

Each moment of our lives, we are choosing what we want and don't want, will and won't do, like and don't like. Daily activity would slow to a crawl if we consciously examined the Hows and Whys behind each choice we make. The signature path is about choosing readily and intuitively.

If you invested heavily in working with the exercises in this chapter, I'd suggest that you put the book aside for a day. Move on to the next chapter when you are fresh and ready to think about another aspect of your self.

CHAPTER THREE

Where Are You Going?

MUCH OF WHAT YOU READ and did in the last chapter, especially your work on the Whys, leads to this question. The Whys may provide life purpose, but that is not the same as having destinations. Where do the Whys lead? What are the destinations along your path that mark and declare its direction? Our arrival at an ultimate destination depends on all of the other stops we make along the way; they lead to where we are going. We will now focus on these interim stops.

EXERCISE

Destination

1. Review what you wrote during the "Hows and Whys" exercise in the last chapter.

2. With these thoughts fresh in your mind, consider what you could do in the short term to

make some of these Whys more apparent in your life. Step down from grand life purposes to the immediate smaller movements toward those life purposes. Consider what you could do in the next year that would support your Whys and list some of those ideas. For example:

"I want to have dinner at home with the family four times this week."

"I want to take a three-week vacation this year."

"I want to work better with Susan and Clarence on the BCD project."

"I want to increase my confidence in dealing with top management."

"I want to read more books on history during the next three months."

3. Your list will be longer and different, but I hope it will share the following qualities with this short list. Your action items:

○ Are obviously related to your Whys.

○ Are immediate and tangible. The list requires actions that you can imagine taking. It is not as abstract and conceptual as your Whys. These are things you could begin to do now if you chose to. This should be appealing to those of you who found the "Hows and Whys" exercise a bit removed from the way you ordinarily approach your life and work.

○ Make up a wide array. There are many ways of reaching out toward your Whys. Present some of those many ways here.

○ Are attractive. List what you really want to do and you are more likely to do something about it.

○ Are outside what you would ordinarily do. This is not the place to list what you are doing anyhow; it is where you note the things that you are not likely to do but really want to. This list is an attempt to alter your priorities, elevating some important Whys in your daily or weekly "to-do" list.

○ Are something you can take action on. There's no point listing things you cannot now or never will be able to do anything about. The list precedes action, so include areas you control or influence. Leave out the rest.

4. From the list, select one item and describe it as a destination. Think of it as a place you want to reach, and write a paragraph about it. Describe what it would be like, its value to you, how it serves your Whys. At this point, do not think about how you might do it; just make it attractive to you. For example, if you were describing a three-week vacation and all of its advantages, you would write about how it connects to your Whys. You would elaborate on what you might do on that vacation and how you and others would benefit from it. You would get specific about when and where you would like to take the vacation. In other words, you would create a mental and written image of the vacation and, by doing so, increase its importance to you. Later in the book, we can worry about others and about gaining their support. Right now, it is enough to express what you want as an achievement, goal, or destination.

Why am I asking you to do all of this thinking about what you could have that you do not have now? The short answer is: to bring it into reality. Already, by writing a paragraph, by describing what you want to create, by imagining it, it has become more real for you. Of course, it is still in the realm of hope and aspiration, but you are more invested in it by thinking of it than by neglecting it. Giving thought to where we want to go makes it more likely that we will get there. No, this is not a casting of magic spells; it makes much more sense than that. For example, if you really want more time with your friends, if you imagine what that could be like, and if you often think about spending time with your friends, all of that wanting and imagining and thinking will make a difference in how you see your world as you move through it each day. Given your heightened consciousness, you are more likely to see and grasp opportunities to be with your friends.

If you want to gain a new skill at work, the same intentionality applies. Prepare yourself to gain the skill by describing for yourself what the skill is and when you would like to have it. Make it a destination that your work path is headed for. Then your path becomes one you are creating rather than one that someone else created and you are just following. Lay the path toward this new work skill by writing to yourself about it: What would you be doing when you reached that point? Who would you be working with? How would others assist you? How would you feel about exercising this skill? What would it require of you? Write a paragraph or a page about this and see how it changes your perception of the world. If what you wrote about and reach for is important to you, you will find connections between that imagined destination and what happens at work. You will ask different questions and speak with different people and your work world will change a little. Or perhaps a lot.

The work of the last two paragraphs needs reinforcement. Describing your destination in specific terms in writing is important because the discipline of writing causes you to concentrate. It also provides you with a record of your thoughts—a record you can return to daily, reminding yourself of this one destination you intend to reach. By returning to the writing, you can hold the destination out in front of you. By reminding you of what you want to do, it will guide you through daily decisions. Opportunities to move toward your destination are more likely to be captured than lost because of your heightened awareness.

You can incorporate this exercise in your life. List the destinations you would like to reach. Select one and describe it in some detail. Remind yourself daily of that destination by reading what you wrote. And watch for opportunities to move toward it. They will be more likely to appear.

Knowing and concentrating on your current destination is a huge advantage in a world full of alternate destinations offered from every shopping mall, pulpit, and television channel. It's not a matter of your being right; it's a matter of knowing where you intend to go.

CHAPTER FOUR

What Do You Need Along the Path?

AS WE MOVE TOWARD WHAT WE WANT in our lives, we carry what we already have. You might imagine all that you have as luggage, or a backpack, perhaps a large wagon, or maybe even a moving van. All that we have accumulated in possessions, habits, patterns, knowledge, talent, wisdom, friendships, pain, joy—all of it moves with us when we move. Imagine yourself moving through the world in that way. Sense the weight, the lightness-to-heaviness of what you have accumulated so far. Notice the effort or ease of moving your accumulations forward with you.

We are going to take a look into all this stuff you are carrying with an eye toward identifying what is important in order to reach the destination you described earlier. Often an inventory of some sort makes sense. The Possessions Chart will help us do that. The quadrants are like four empty boxes into which you can sort what you have and need to reach your destination, wherever that might be. These boxes help you to see what you have accumulated and find what's really essential. A few words about each quadrant before putting you to work:

Possessions Chart

	Not Have	Have
Need	**II**	**I**
Not Need	**IV**	**III**

Quadrant I, "Need and Have," shows the support you have for reaching your destination, what you need and have to make this trip. For example, if your destination is to reconsider work's place in your life, this book might be in your "Need and Have" box. You might turn to this upper right quadrant for reassurance because it contains the skills, the attitudes, the learning, and the resources that you already have to make this trip.

Quadrant II, "Need and Not Have," is a quadrant of vulnerability. Not having something you need does not mean that you cannot begin the trip; it just means that it will be harder, or you will have to acquire what is needed along the way, or you must live with the consequences of not having it. For example, though you might "Need and Have" this book to help you reconsider work's place in your life, you may "Need and Not Have" the time for this thoughtful reconsideration. That will hamper you.

Quadrant III, "Not Need and Have," is all the stuff you can put aside as excess baggage. Most journeys in life are like our vacations: we pack a lot more than we will ever use and expend a great deal of energy carrying what we do not need. For example, if you have purchased five books about work-life balance and have not read them, I'd suggest that they may look nice on your bookshelf, but you do not need all of them.

Quadrant IV, "Not Need and Not Have," is like the stuff advertised in airline magazines and on shopping channels. This is all the stuff that you haven't acquired and can get along without. If we were to pile up all the potential acquisitions in this box, they would be 148 stories high, dwarfing the other three boxes. This pile, by definition, is physically absent but calls out to us; it tries to fool us into moving it to one of the two "Need" quadrants. Its contents are best dealt with by saying aloud, "I don't need it and I don't want it!" An additional challenge you might rise to is to ask yourself how you can move some stuff from the "Not Need and Have" box to the "Not Need and Not Have" box.

You can use this model in relation to your life destination. Everything you have and know can be sorted into one of these four quadrants. Asking yourself to do this might provoke some useful thought and action, but for the moment, our purposes are more modest. We are going to use the model on one of those interim destinations you listed in the last chapter—the one you described in a paragraph.

Possessions

1. Get out the paragraph you wrote earlier that describes one of your current life destinations. Read it and absorb it; return yourself to a full appreciation of this destination that you wish to reach. After about five minutes of reminding yourself, . . .

2. Draw four large boxes in your journal or on a separate piece of paper to represent the four quadrants. You might be tempted to set aside your garage or family room for this, but please don't. What you need is a place to collect ideas, not a place to collect objects you own. Provide yourself with lots

of room to write down your thoughts. This is where you are going to identify the resources you need to reach your current destination.

3. Now begin to sort your possessions, keeping your destination in mind. Start with more tangible possessions like tools, vehicles, money, time, clothing, and people. Move on to less tangible, but potentially valuable, possessions like technical skills, natural talent, personal qualities or attributes, confidence, and anxiety. Invest at least ten minutes in doing this, then put it aside for a couple of hours, if you have the time.

4. Don't take this exercise too seriously. Remind yourself that this is a way of thinking differently about what you want from the world. These different thoughts and this new perspective might shake loose some alternatives you have not thought about before.

5. Read the descriptions of each of the boxes again and look at what you have put in each box so far. When you think you are ready, . . .

6. Move on to action. Stand back and look at all you have done, the descriptive paragraph about the destination plus the four filled-out boxes. If you were going to do something to further your journey along your path to your current destination, what might it be? Generate a list of possible actions with *no* commitment to taking any of them. You are not deciding now; you are generating alternatives for later decisions. Come up with eight to twelve alternatives.

7. From these alternatives, select at least one to act upon. Select an action that you really want to take, that will move you toward your destination, that is likely to make some difference, and that is different from what you have done so far. Highlight or mark the action in some way. Refine its expression so that you know clearly what you are to do, when you intend to do it, and why you are going to do it.

8. Do it.

CHAPTER FIVE

Your Three Selves

MANY ATHLETES COMMENT on the internal calm they experience while they are achieving a personal best. You have probably heard them express what they felt inside while performing. You may know the joy of developing a talent that you can use without thinking about it, without conscious guidance. The talent pours from you naturally. And in the middle of performing, you can watch yourself perform. This awareness, this self-observing while performing, is present in these examples:

○ A tennis player forgets trying to do what her coach told her to do and just does it. She achieves a state of mind in which she quits thinking about how to play tennis. She just lets her body play, while she watches herself play.

○ A very busy man lies down and lets his body go to sleep. As his whirring thoughts drop into the background, they become like voices in another room. He is aware of their leaving and of the diffused focus that is in the foreground. He watches and feels his body preparing for sleep and falling asleep.

○ A project leader listens to a point of view that is quite different from his own. He is aware of putting his own thoughts on a high shelf in his mind while he takes in the new ideas. He does this intentionally, calmly, holding his thoughts "up here" while accepting those being put in front of him.

○ A woman converses with a friend. At the same time, she is aware of herself from outside the conversation, watching the two of them talk even as she is talking. This watching self is calmer and more removed than the animated, engaged self.

 Make a short written or mental list of what these four examples have in common. They look, and are, quite different in terms of the actual, physical performance involved and the surroundings. They would look even more different if we did not have the advantage of seeing what is going on in these people's minds.

To your list, you might add these common characteristics:

○ Performance of a physically observable activity
○ Engagement in performing a developed talent
○ Significant internal, mental activity
○ Awareness of what the physical and mental selves are doing
○ Detachment from the performing self
○ Calm emanating from the more detached self

Compare these characteristics to those on your own list.

But who is doing all of this? It is beginning to sound as if more than one self is present. How many selves might each of us have? Consider the possibility that at least three selves are present in each of these examples and in each of us—a public self, a private self, and a reflective self.

The *public self* is the physical, acting, observable, external self. It exists from our skin out and includes everything we hang on it to represent us, like clothing, scents, and accessories; it even reaches out to include vehicles. It has to do with image and perception, with the meaning of self that we are trying to create for ourselves and to present to others. We all give time to this public self because it is where we touch and receive the world. Our intentions and aspirations actually reach the world through our public self. The public self treads our signature path with guidance from inside.

The *private self* lies behind the public self. This second self accesses the outside world through the public self's five senses. It sees through the eyes, hears through the ears, and so on; it then acts on all that collected information. It operates from somewhere within the skin and controls the public self—or at least it attempts to. At this moment, your observable public self appears to be reading a book while your private self reacts to and makes meaning of the stream of words coming in through your eyes.

The *reflective self* watches and guides the interplay between the public and private selves and it learns. Figuratively, this third self is sitting on a ledge at some height, outside of and slightly above the exchange between the public and private selves. From this perspective, the reflective self is calmer and quieter than the other selves. It makes meaning of what it sees—actions, associations, the moment, life. This observing self witnesses the congruities and incongruities between the other two selves. It considers life as it has been, is, and could be.

For example, while your public self holds, sees, and reads this page, your private self might be saying, "Yes, this fits with what I know." "How does this fit with what I learned years back about extroverts and introverts?" "I like what he has to say." Your private self carries on this internal stream-of-consciousness dialogue based on what the public self feeds it from the external world. At the same time, your reflective self makes quieter, less frequent observations of the other two selves. As your public self is reading and your private self is assessing what comes in, your reflective self might be saying something like "You reveal a pattern of inquiry and learning in your life" or "You regularly try to build on your life's experience." Okay, so it sounds a little bit like a Chinese fortune cookie, but that is the role the reflective self aspires to: being thoughtful, profound, patient, and wise. Its reflective role means that it will speak less often than the private self.

Finding Your Selves

Let's apply these notions of public self, private self, and reflective self to a common situation from your life. And what is more common for many of us than

EXERCISE

meetings? Here is a process for increasing awareness of what you are doing:

1. Before going further, on a sheet of paper or in your journal, divide a page into three columns with two vertical lines. Label the columns from left to right: "Public Self," "Private Self," and "Reflective Self," like this:

Public Self	Private Self	Reflective Self

    You are going to be filling in these columns as you work through this process. In doing so, you will have help from my friend, Patricia, who offers her completed columns as a guide for you.

2. Start by thinking about a specific meeting you attended recently, a meeting in which you were actively, willingly involved. Recall what you did—your observable behavior, your public self—during the meeting. What would a videotape of the meeting have captured? Under the "Public Self" column, note what you did during the meeting that could have been observed on the videotape. To illustrate, here is an example from Patricia, who wrote about these specific actions:

Public Self	Private Self	Reflective Self
Introduced a new idea to the team assembled		
Participated very actively		
Built on the ideas others offered		
Changed my opinion on one point		

Resisted changing
on two other
points

Interjected humor

Related back to the
history of the
organization

Asked a summariz-
ing, concluding
question

If you had been there, you would have seen Patricia take
each of those actions. As she recalled the meeting, it came
back to life for her. The same can happen for you when you
think back on your meeting. In the "Public Self" column,
list six to eight actions that others could see you take during the meeting.

3. Next, look down your "Public Self" list and recall the
   thoughts and feelings you had while taking the actions, especially reactions that you did not share with others, but kept
   to yourself. Write these in the column labeled "Private Self."
   Take a look at how Patricia did this, then do it for yourself:

Public Self	Private Self	Reflective Self
Introduced a new idea to the team assembled	See how quick and creative I am!	
Participated very actively	Look at me!	
Built on the ideas others offered	Everybody should get involved.	
Changed my opin-ion on one point	I am open to others. See how flexible I am!	
Resisted changing on two other points	Hear and under-stand what I have to say.	
Interjected humor	Let's lighten up— and aren't I funny?	
Related back to the history of the organization	I have history and power here.	

Asked a summarizing, concluding question	I want to influence what this team focuses on.

Notice that Patricia's inner reflections are offered as "I" statements. Her private self is expressing what it is seeking through the actions of the public self. Her example is a good one for you to consider. The "Private Self" column need not include everything you thought and felt, just highlights. Look deeply enough into your private self to express what you're thinking and feeling, then write it down.

4. As you look down your "Public Self" and "Private Self" columns, what patterns do you see? Search through the two columns for underlying larger purposes. For example, when Patricia looked at her purposes behind her actions and feelings, she detected a pattern of attempting to have her uniqueness recognized. Her work looks like this:

Public Self	Private Self	Reflective Self
Introduced a new idea to the team assembled	See how quick and creative I am!	*She regularly draws attention to herself.*
Participated very actively	Look at me!	
Built on the ideas others offered	Everybody should get involved.	*Her ego often gets in the way of contribution.*
Changed my opinion on one point	I am open to others. See how flexible I am!	*She tries in many ways to influence the group.*
Resisted changing on two other points	Hear and understand what I have to say.	*She consistently works toward making something happen.*
Interjected humor	Let's lighten up— and aren't I funny?	
Related back to the history of the organization	I have history and power here.	
Asked a summarizing, concluding question	I want to influence what this team focuses on.	

Do the same with your "Public Self" and "Private Self" columns as Patricia has done. In the "Reflective Self" column, write down patterns you observe in the first two columns. Use the third person ("he" or "she"), as Patricia did. This reinforces the notion that you are trying to observe yourself from a point outside your public and private selves. Look in the "Public Self" and "Private Self" columns for at least three patterns in your behaviors or intentions during this meeting. Your statements about patterns are written in the "Reflective Self" column because that is just what you have been doing, reflecting. And they are fewer because they reflect patterns of behavior or intention.

It is this third column that we have been building to: your reflective self. The reflective self watches what you are doing on the outside and listens in on what you are thinking and feeling inside. It learns from what it sees and remembers what it has learned for later use. It creates its own meaning from watching the public and private selves as they cooperate to make an impact on the outside world. The more aware you are of your reflective self, the better use you can make of it.

In the exercise, we drew on the reflective self's more immediate coaching capability. It extracted meaning out of what it saw going on between the public and private selves at a meeting and developed wisdom from the patterns it observed. But the reflective self is more than a coach for the other selves. Of the three, it stands closest to a life perspective. The reflective self is the least expedient one; it makes time to think about how all of your current actions fit with your past actions and future intentions. Based on its experience with your life, it assesses where you are as well as where you are going. Its vocabulary includes such words as *values, future, vision, will, wisdom, choice,* and *intention.* This is your most thoughtful and centered self. In it, over time, you ponder your meaning and purpose. The reflective self offers the other selves perspective, patience, and balance. It guides your life—when you are quiet enough to hear its guidance. The other selves are much busier and noisier; they need the centering that the reflective self can bring.

The role of the reflective self will become even clearer in future chapters. In one sense, this entire book is an encouragement to seek and develop your reflective self and to follow its guidance along your signature path.

Consider the potential importance of the notion of the reflective self and describe it in your journal in your own words. How do you distinguish it from everything else that is going on inside of you? What has it done, might it do, for you? What are you learning as you think about the three selves discussed here?

Seeing Your Public and Private Selves

Many of us yield to the enticements of images created for us by others. The media and its sponsors bombard our self-image. They know what we could be—if we used their products. The images they hold up for us to embrace can only be achieved temporarily, after eighteen takes, under perfect lighting, and at considerable expense. They are not something you and I are likely to realize the first time around. Their images are about surfaces. What you see in a mirror is the outside of what you have to work with. What you see is important, but not nearly as important as all you cannot see that is behind the eyes looking back at you from that mirror.

This exercise asks you to look at yourself in the mirror to help you see your selves better. Start by reading the following six steps. If they seem strange to you, I would *especially* encourage you to do the exercise. Read over the six steps; note their main elements (look, breathe, notice, speak, act, and reflect) so you don't have to refer back to these pages. Here's the process:

1. Find a private place with a mirror large enough to reflect your face.
2. Stand (or sit) in front of the mirror and look. Just look into those eyes looking back at you. Scattered or centered, happy or sad, tidy or messy. Look. Look and breathe. Let your eyes rest on the reflection of that person who is so essential to

you. Look and breathe slowly and deeply. Don't do anything but look and breathe.

3. As you do this, thoughts and feelings will flicker across your mind and heart. Notice them; don't hold onto them. Let them go by. Continue to look and breathe for at least three minutes.

4. After quietly looking at your reflection, watching yourself breathe, and noticing your thoughts and feelings, speak to this person you have been so attentive to. Say whatever comes to your mind. At least say it silently. Maybe say it aloud. And notice the effect of speaking to yourself. Repeat what you have said and notice the effect of doing that.

5. Take one last look at your reflection; look away and leave the mirror.

6. Think about what you want to do next. How did your short time alone inform what you want to do next? How do you feel about what you are going to do next? How do those feelings compare to how you felt before looking at yourself in the mirror?

This little exercise produces a wide array of effects on people. Here are a few reactions: "It was the quietest part of my whole day." "I should do this more often." "I felt a connection to myself that I want to keep." "The whole thing made me uncomfortable, I mean, what was supposed to happen?" "After about a minute, I started to cry and I'm still not sure why." "It sounds stupid but I got a little scared." "A huge feeling of love and self-confidence swept through me." "It was like someone was looking at me who knows me well and feels sorry for me." "I'm going to do this again!"

JOURNAL

Such comments may or may not fit with your experience. What *you* experienced is what counts. What stirred in you? What did this look at yourself cause to happen? What feelings? thoughts? movement? What did you learn about yourself in this short time? Note your responses to these questions in your journal. Your reflection knows more about who you are than others ever will.

What you just experienced through the mirror has a great deal to do with your public, private, and reflective selves. Think about it: Which self were you seeing as you started your first minute of looking at your reflection? As time went on and you felt inner stirrings of thoughts and feelings, which self were you seeing then? Could you detect any other self standing back a bit from the mirror and observing the process that was under way? My hope is that you were aware of your public, private, and reflective selves while you were looking in the mirror, especially your public and private selves. Initially, the mirror reflects back the same image that other people see on meeting you. This is the self you present to the world. But as you look longer and more deeply, the private self begins to reshape the face in front of you. Changes in the face express meanings that are not initially apparent; these changes are likely to be accompanied by internal feelings and thoughts held by the private self. The public and private selves may move toward becoming one.

You may have had a parallel experience as you were looking into the eyes of a friend. Recall times when you and another person have held each other's eyes for what felt like a long time. Remember how your eyes and faces changed; recall the feelings that accompanied this deeper contact. We seldom look into another person's eyes without being deeply stirred. The emotions vary, but the stirring is almost always there, calling out questions about who we are and what we are presenting to the other person at this moment. The stirring relates to our own authenticity, to whether we are being truly and deeply present. Our friendship calls on us to align our public and private selves in our relationship with the other person.

CHAPTER SIX

Higher Views
of Self

BEFORE DIVING INTO THIS CHAPTER, I want to remind us why we are going through all of these exercises. We are in the middle of doing the subtitle of this book, "Gaining New Perspectives on Life and Work." The subtitle does not read "Gaining *the One True* Perspective . . ." I am attempting to engage you in seeing in new ways. Each of the exercises moves us to a new viewpoint in our mind from which we look out at what surrounds us, like the signs along the highway that say, "Scenic Point 500 Yards." My focus is not on getting you to complete the exercises or fill your journal with notes, or on either of us being right. Instead, I am focused on helping you to see what happens along the way during an exercise, or to recognize the feelings and thoughts you have while writing, or to notice your concern (or lack of it) about doing it right. Through my words and these exercises, I am trying to create experiences in new perspectives for you. I made up everything that is here with the intent of engaging your mind in seeing differently. If you are getting new ideas and insights, the book is working. If you are not, try to stay open to the possibility that there just might be something here. Now the chapter begins.

The reflective self took on some special roles and responsibilities in the last chapter. The more patient, wise, and centered part of you, the reflective self has great potential as an internal guide through your life. It sees from a higher viewpoint than the more immediate public self, or the more protective and reactive private self. We need all three selves to get through life, but the observing reflective self, which is much needed in the world, is easiest to neglect. The rest of this chapter helps you to consider your reflective self more deeply. It assists you in answering the following questions: If there is a reflective self, where is it watching from? What opinions does it hold? How does it process what it observes? How does it influence your life?

EXERCISE

Four Sweet Views

In this exercise, you will be looking at four ways to measure yourself. The exercise emerged one morning over a long breakfast with friends in an elegant hotel garden. It was the sugar and sweetener packets on the table that gave me the idea. If you want to fully honor the moment of creation, you will need to acquire nine white sugar packets, nine blue sweetener packets, and nine pink sweetener packets. Those packets, in various combinations, gave the exercise its name, "Four Sweet Views." Don't rush off to borrow packets from your neighborhood restaurant; my drawings and your notes will work just fine.

I am going to offer four views of ourselves, four ways we can measure ourselves as we go through life. We are not as simple as "good" and "bad," but these views will talk about us in that way, for the sake of making the four alternatives clear. Read each view, try it on, and notice its effect on you. Some views will fit better than others; some will attract you more. Notice all of that, too, and keep your journal handy.

View One: Split

This first view requires two blue packets and one pink packet. Lay them out as shown in the first figure. If you are doing this at work, it might be a bit hard to explain, but do it anyhow. What the hell, tell them you are deeply involved in self-development! Select packets of one color to stand for all that you value in yourself and packets of the other color to stand for the oppo-

 site. In the first view, we are showing a clear separation of what you value and don't value in yourself.

When we see the world through this view, we are inclined to focus on what we value about ourselves and to deny or sublimate or hide what we don't value. We separate our "good" and "bad" sides intentionally. We don't want others to know about our bad side; we often don't want to know much about it ourselves. We feel ashamed of our bad behavior and may deny it to ourselves as well as others. We believe we have a lot to hide and protect.

So that is one view. Does it fit with how you experience yourself? What would be different about your life if you saw yourself this way? Use some paper or your journal to make a few notes about View One. Don't come to any firm conclusions; you've got three more views ahead of you.

Now that you have seen one view, let's take a paragraph to discuss the reflective self's role in all four views. It is the reflective self that chooses between these four viewpoints or creates its own. A key question for the reflective self is, "How do I see myself in the world?" The answer to the question yields a description, and behind the description are some assumptions. These four views illustrate four sets of assumptions. For example, View One includes these assumptions: "I have two sides." "They are separate and it is important to keep them separate." "I want to show one side; I want to hide the other." The position of the packets illustrates this separation simply and distinguishes this first view from the others.

The larger point is that these views are alternatives for the reflective self. Each view has consequences when we use it. Our views determine what our public self pays attention to in the world and what we do with it once we get it inside our private self. The reflective self provides frameworks to contain and guide what the other two selves do. On to View Two.

View Two: Mix

The second view requires another two blue packets and another pink packet. Lay them down as I've shown here, with the one pink packet overlapping the two blue ones. This represents quite a different self-assessment from the one in View One. Here both sides of the self are acknowledged, overlapping, and constantly present in the person. When we see ourselves this way, we believe that we are a combination of what we value and do not value in ourselves. Our intention is to integrate the two. A more accurate representation of this view would be to tear the blue and pink packets into small pieces, pour their contents together, and stir them. This view mixes bad and good qualities together; each is a part of the other.

People with this view of themselves are more likely to acknowledge their array of behaviors and to intentionally and comfortably display them. For example, they are more likely to acknowledge a bad temper or a disorderly nature or a lack of abil-

ity. They are also more likely to acknowledge their talents. They display their spectrum of qualities more than a person speaking out of View One. Can you find this view in yourself? Notice how this view fits you or doesn't fit you. Considering Views One and Two, which is more like

you most of the time? How do you demonstrate this? What would be different about your life if you saw yourself this way? Make some notes before moving on.

View Three: Net

View Three is a net game: I have these qualities I value in myself; they total two packets. I have these qualities that take away from my good side; they total one packet. The net result is one positive packet. Two minus one equals one. When we operate out of this framework, we keep track of both sides of ourselves, like good bookkeepers. We see the two sides as separate but related. In this third view, we are willing to acknowledge our positive and negative sides, but we really focus on the end result. What counts is to net out positive. Negative points reduce the positive total that was possible. Speaking as a "net one positive" person, you might say, "Sure, I did a good job on the presentation, about a plus seven on a ten-point scale. But I didn't handle the discussion well at all—it was about a minus two. So I net out at about a plus five, which is okay." Now, is View Three a fit for you? What would be different about your life if you saw yourself

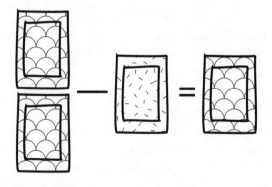

this way? Compare this view to the first two. Which is most like you? Make a few notes before continuing.

When we act within the first view, we present some parts of ourselves and hide or deny others. Within the second view, we express the whole mixed stew that is us. And in the third view, we seek to balance our internal ledger on the credit side by ensuring that the net result is more good than bad. Can you see how these three perspectives affect actions we take on our signature path? The ways we frame ourselves determine how we affect what is around us, how we contribute, and how we assess our contribution. Each view suggests a different approach to self-assessment, action, and personal growth.

View Four: Hold

In this view, what we have been calling the good and bad sides of a person stand separately, but they are held together by their common background. No attempt is made to split them, mix them, or net them out. Each side stands separate from but in relation to the other. The white background in my drawing stands for the awareness and bound-

aries of the reflective self, boundaries that accept and hold all the parts in creative relationship with each other. In View Four, we can speak authentically from any part of ourselves, but always providing the larger context of our whole person. How does this fourth view fit with how you ordinarily see yourself? Can you see the difference between this view and the other three? It is a harder concept to express, grasp, and hold—and it is worth holding.

For example, you might say, "I am giving my most negative opinions about this recommendation right now. I also have positive opinions, but I am not presenting them at this moment." Note that you are acknowledging both sides but are only speaking to one at the moment. When we operate with a View Four framework, we are more likely to hold internal conflicts and contradictions without feeling the need to resolve them. We keep them in creative tension, spinning around each other, and we value these internal tensions. We might recognize that we keep a tidy office and a messy garage and feel no need to be consistent.

Or we might be frugal with grocery money and buy expensive cars or computers that we don't really need.

Can you find this part of yourself? It is a newer view to many and it is not reinforced much at work. This fourth view offers more self-acceptance and appreciation of ourselves as we are. When we are successful in seeing the world through this fourth view, life is easier because of our acceptance of paradox and contradiction. But gaining and living that acceptance of differences inside and outside ourselves requires great faith in this fourth, all-inclusive framework.

The four views—Split, Mix, Net, and Hold—offer frameworks through which the reflective self can filter its observations. The filter itself is what we have been trying to emphasize. As you look out on the world around you, as you react to the signals you are receiving, as you consider who you are becoming, all of this information is sorted and stored within some kind of framework. This framework is often more important than the information it contains. The framework is developed and maintained by the reflective self, with its underlying assumptions about you, your world, and your path. (See the Four Sweet Views chart.)

Perhaps, through working with these four views, your own view has become clearer. With your journal in hand, consider these questions:

o How do you process, sort, and store the information you are holding about yourself?

o Where do you keep what you value more and less about yourself?

o How aware are you of a reflective self with a framework?

o If you were to draw your version of a framework, what would it look like?

o Having worked through the four views, what would you like to learn more about? How will you do this?

As potentially wise and informed as the reflective self is, it is by no means a neutral third party. In its patient and ever-attentive way, it is always collecting information about you

Four Sweet Views

View		I: Split	II: Mix	III: Net	IV: Hold
Orientation:		Separation	Combination	Result	Inclusion
Strength:		Focus on positive self	Rich, creative ideas Array of feelings	Focus on positive end product	Open to all views
Weakness:		Denial of negative self	Ideas and feelings mixed, not sorted	End product is all that counts	Appears contradictory and in conflict with self
Comment:		Smile and hide	Let it all hang out!	Destination, not the journey	Knows all parts of self

through your other selves. It observes what your public and private selves are doing and has to decide what to do with that information. So it builds its patterns, frameworks, and prejudices. And these become the way you see yourself and your world. You just explored four of many possible ways of seeing yourself.

CHAPTER SEVEN

Your Shadow Knows

"WHAT EVIL LURKS IN THE HEARTS OF MEN? The Shadow knows." Some of you "pre-Boomers" will recall the weekly radio drama that began with those lines. Many years later, I am discovering greater depth and meaning in those lines than Lamont Cranston (The Shadow) ever intended when he spoke them.

The shadow does lurk within each of us, the shadow of those unacknowledged, unwanted, unknown, unexplored, and denied sides of ourselves. The shadow is there as surely as our revealed and more enlightened selves. It does "lurk" because that is the nature of the work we have assigned it to do. And it is important to our development. For some of us, it holds the most potential for growth. There's lots of good news in the shadow! At least that is how we will approach the shadow in this chapter.

The shadow is the side of the self on which we have not yet shined a light. This lack of light leaves us ignorant of a part of ourselves. Our shadow side is not necessarily good or bad, or virtuous or wicked; it is mostly unknown. Depending on where you are going, shining a light into your own shadow could make sense—not using a searchlight, and not looking in every corner all at once, but lighting up the edges a bit at a time.

Many of us have given years to concentrating on our more positive selves. In the last chapter, the view called "Split" fits with the public self we have presented. We build on our strengths using what we know well. This positive approach is rewarded by others. It is admirable and upbeat; it fits with American culture and mythology. But as wonderful as it is, it is only part of the path toward our potential. The shadowy parts of the path are just as rich as, and some say even richer than, the fully lighted portions. Most of us venture onto these paths with less intention than will be suggested here. We often happen upon the shadow in the process of doing something else, frequently around the middle of life. Some link does seem to exist between awareness of our shadow and awareness of our mortality. When the shadow appears, it is not easy to brush it aside; it looms as a mysterious, compelling, internal place.

So how can you begin to look for what might be tucked away in your shadow? Think back on how you have learned about yourself in the past. What allowed you to learn to see yourself differently? Often, learning about yourself comes from a change of situation. Somehow, some way, circumstances changed to give you information about yourself that you did not have before. For example, your boss described your performance in terms that were radically different from how you saw yourself, or a friend was highly critical of you. These experiences suggest a starting point. Learn about your shadow by turning toward it and opening yourself to what you see. That is what we will do now in an exercise called "Lighting the Shadows." Approach it with a sense of fun and daring.

Lighting the Shadows

EXERCISE

1. Start with a clean page in your journal. Head the page with one of these phrases:

   "What I am afraid of is . . ."

   "What I am ashamed of is . . ."

   "What I am embarrassed about is . . ."

   "What I am uncomfortable having others know is . . ."

   Select one of these or make one up. We will use "What I am afraid of is . . ." as our example in the exercise.

2. Now begin listing possible completions for the sentence. Let go and write down everything you think of that might fit under the heading—bees, spiders, the dark, Democrats, telephones in the night. Just keep writing. Don't worry whether you are getting it right. Nobody is going to see this list but you. Try to fill the page with things and events—a heart attack, drowning, airplanes, tunnels. Just keep writing—electric shock, liverwurst, elevator shafts, Republicans, icy roads. When you start running out of the easier fears, move to the more complicated ones—when the boss calls and asks me to come down to her office, when my mate gets upset with me. You get the idea; just keep writing. Really delve into your corners and your past. Spend at least five minutes doing this, filling the page if you can.

3. Read back through the page. First, underline the top five things that are especially fearful (or embarrassing or shaming or uncomfortable) to you.

4. Circle and draw lines connecting all the fears on the page that you think could be related, that seem to be connected to similar persons, places, things, or feelings. Imagine that these fears are connected in more ways than just by being within you. What else might connect them? Spend time looking for connections. Make up or try out these connections. Notice the feelings you have while you are doing this. Be especially aware of any feelings of discomfort that seem to be related to the connections you are drawing on the page.

5. Next, ask yourself, why? Why are these items underlined? Why are those items circled? Why did I connect these two things? On a fresh page, write down some of your answers. Notice any new thoughts that come up in the process, especially thoughts you have not given much credence to before. Note them. Also notice your feelings while you are exploring these Whys, especially feelings of excitement, discomfort, anxiety, or discovery. This exercise is intended to encourage discovery. Is that happening? Are you open to it? Capture any new realizations.

6. Notice your attempts to block your thoughts. Are you thinking, "I don't want to be doing this!" or "Enough. I've gone far enough. I quit!" If so, go ahead; quit. But first ask, "Why do I not want to do this?" Write down your answer, and ask yourself why your reason is important to you. You may find some shadowy clues there. Notice what your mind wants to do instead of thinking about this shadowy task. Notice where your mind runs to. Use your reflective self to observe what you do instead of bringing some small part of yourself out into the light. These are more clues. The shadow lurks around the edges of your discomfort; it often creates that discomfort. So if you want to learn about it, you don't have to go far.

7. As you finish this exploration, ask yourself what you learned by working through it. Jot down some of those things, however grand or humble they might be.

Visiting the edges of our shadow side requires moving into intentional discomfort. But there is no reason this visit should be comfortable. We are approaching unfamiliar terrain, and discomfort is part of the process. If you are not uncomfortable during the process, the chances are that you have not looked far from the lighted path. Looking in the shadow is not an essential step each of us must take on our signature path. Those of us who find ourselves regularly blocked from progressing to what we want in life may find reasons in our shadow side. Life energy and power can be freed in the discovery and acceptance of these hidden parts of ourselves.

Getting your shadow out into the light allows you to meet it more constructively and openly. Use these techniques:

○ Acknowledge and respect the shadow's existence.

○ Move toward it, learn more about it, and gradually shed light on it.

○ Accept that you are hiding parts of yourself from yourself.

○ Name the shadowy parts of yourself that you can acknowledge.

○ Talk with trusted friends about the process you are engaging in—about what you are doing and feeling, and with what purpose. Ask them to read this chapter, and discuss it with them.

○ Reveal to friends something from your shadow that you have not revealed before. Note their reactions and your reactions to doing this. When these reactions are encouraging, reveal more.

○ Notice the impact on your self-image, self-confidence, and authenticity that comes with knowing more about yourself.

○ Review your journal notes from the exercise "Seeing Your Public and Private Selves" in Chapter Five and look for links to what you have noted since.

○ Incorporate newly discovered parts of yourself in the ways you think about yourself and describe yourself to others.

○ Know that the shadow will always be there and will never be fully revealed to you. What you moved into the light is connected to another part of you that you have yet to discover.

Your work with your shadow can affect the people around you. As you change in small ways, your changes will affect them. When others see or hear what you are doing, their reactions to what you are doing will range from puzzled to amazed, and they may ask you about it. Some people will tell you that you are dealing with the issues they have been reluctant to acknowledge in their own lives. The most personal growth issues are usually the most widely felt. For example, in an exercise with forty consultants, we discovered that over half of the consultants had frequent, significant doubts about their professional abilities but that they only rarely acknowledged this to anyone. Most of us were amazed to find that this anxiety was so widely shared. People usually respect your openness. They may acknowledge that you have spoken their secrets. And some of them will go back through their shadowy closets and attics to bring out their own neglected or denied selves.

Your World

O world invisible, we view thee,

O world intangible, we touch thee,

O world unknowable, we know thee.

—FRANCIS THOMPSON

A NOUN IS A PERSON, PLACE, OR THING, but do you remember what a gerund is? A gerund is a verbal noun. According to one dictionary definition, it is "the *-ing* form of a verb when functioning as a noun." These two definitions may seem like a strange way to begin Part Two, but they are very much to the point. Part Two asks you to see your world as a verbal noun, to see your world as "worlding." We each choose how we see the world around us. Part Two is about an active, emerging world that you participate in creating.

We are very reassured by seeing the world as a noun. The static, reliable, defined nature of a noun has a dependability about it. This rock, that mountain, this company. We can count on nouns when we need certainty! Contrast nouns with gerunds. Gerunds are those "-ing" words like *singing, analyzing, mowing, dreaming, thinking,* and *fishing.* Gerunds are attractive in their movement. They are busy. They are not done; they are doing. Notice the difference between *talk* and *talking,* between *work* and *working, dance* and *dancing, balance* and *balancing, love* and *loving, life* and *living.* Gerunds engage us in quite a different way from nouns. They are active and vital; they are becoming.

This world, expressed as a verbal noun, is *worlding.* The world is creating itself in every moment, and creating us with it. And we are creating ourselves, becoming ourselves in every moment. In doing so, we are participating in creating the world. Each moment, we are choosing what we are being. Whether we are acting, hating, speaking, loving, listening, gesturing, running, or analyzing, we are clearly verbal nouns. Dynamic and in process. Our continually unfinished state requires choosing, redirecting, assessing, deciding, learning, and growing all along the way. We are never done; we are always doing.

What does this emerging-world perspective do to the "answers" you find? What does it do to the ideas you put forth? Everything becomes conditional; imagine "So far, . . ." put in front of every assertion. "So far, we have learned this" or "So far, I can't see why that would be true" or "That is important to me, so far." What happens to our certainty? What happens to our convictions? Knowing that we are answering, rather than having the answer, moves us into an unending searching and answering mode. This is not a world where the lines are drawn clearly, where the truth can be found easily, where resolution means completion. This is a world full of questioning, answering, emerging, and constant learning.

The chapters in Part Two are about your world, your communities, and your roles. These four chapters help you to think about the height, breadth, and depth of your world, as well as about the many communities you are willingly (and reluctantly) part of. You will be thinking about the roles you want to play and the extent to which those roles serve you and serve others.

CHAPTER EIGHT

What Does Your World Include?

WE GRAPPLE WITH THE WORLD; we often struggle with what it offers us. At home, at work, at play, at rest, reality creeps up and disrupts the life we imagined we would lead. The world often insists that we take action that is quite different from what we expected, planned, or believed we deserve. We find ourselves reacting when we had hoped to be in charge. Sometimes we conclude, reluctantly, that the world is beyond our understanding and control. This chapter centers on an exercise that offers you ways to accept the world as it comes to you. It starts with a card table and builds your world upon that small table. "Thought-bites" are offered throughout the exercise to stimulate your thinking. Albert Einstein said that imagination is more important than knowledge. With that inspiration, let's begin.

The Tabletop

1. Imagine a bare card table and draw it on a clean page of your journal. Imagine this small table as the place where you are going to pile everything in the world.

2. Now imagine collecting all that you know, feel, do, believe, and value and placing it on this table. Take your work, your family, your friends, your community, your childhood, your beliefs, your politics, your dark secrets, yourself. Put them all on the tabletop. Take your shoe size, your illnesses, your refrigerator, your philosophy of life, your travel plans, your loves, your social security number, and your Visa bill. Everything you can think of or imagine is here on this tabletop, all piled up. It's crowded, it's confusing, but it's all here.

   Now that you have piled up this hodgepodge of the experiences, belongings, perspectives, toys, beliefs, material goods, convictions, prejudices, knowledge, fears, talents, and relationships that make up "you," there should be nothing left elsewhere. Every bit of you is there, on the table. Picture this as clearly as you can. With pencil and paper, represent all this stuff on the table that you drew earlier. And, for good measure, put yourself on top.

3. Imagine that this heaped-up table is standing in the middle of a room. Create a strong mental picture of yourself and all that is you, on the table, in the middle of a room. Pause to visualize this and/or to draw it. When you have got it, move on.

4. Describe the room. Where is the table in the room? What does the room look like? How large is it? What is not on the table, but in the room? Look around. What else is in the room? Write down some of the possibilities. Draw the room and some of the possibilities you have imagined.

   Some of you are saying, "What does he mean, What *else* is in the room?" If this little exercise seems silly to you, you are right: it is silly—to you. Accept and reach beyond this discomfort. This could be part of your path toward something important, or at least different. This exercise might have value, too. And if it doesn't, you have lost little.

5. Consider these possibilities for what is in the room but not on the table, and add them to your own list:
   o Everything you don't know about
   o Everything you haven't yet learned about that affects you
   o Everything you know about that you have chosen not to remember or include
   o Everything you are hiding from
   o Everything that has yet to happen to you
   o Everything from the past that has influenced you but that you are unaware of
   o Every alternative way of understanding and seeing what you have not put on the table

Read over the above list again and add to your list anything important that you may have missed. By listing what is not on your table, you move it onto the table too. The short list above represents everything that you haven't heard about, or haven't learned, or don't believe in, or blind yourself to, or deny, or haven't gotten around to yet. It covers all that you have yet to make part of your world. This list is your search for the realities that you have not yet found and put on the table. You don't know or use what's on this list because you cannot; none of it is on the table. You cannot work with what you haven't got.

An example comes to mind: Bruce worked for a telecommunications company for twenty-three years. He was fortunate to have had wonderful work, to have moved steadily up, and to have worked with great people. Bruce just lost his job through the latest downsizing of his company. Despite the warnings, earlier downsizings, and all of the anxiety at his company, Bruce never seriously considered for a minute that he would lose his job. He had planned at least fifteen more years with this company. The possibility of being let go was not on his table. As a result, Bruce is taking his job loss extremely hard—harder than many other people in the same straits. His world did not include this possibility and he won't be able to move forward until he accepts the reality of what happened.

6. When the world brings something to you that is not on your tabletop, what do you do with it? Here are a few of your choices:

   ○ Accept it and expand your world; put it on your tabletop.

   ○ Ignore it and attempt to maintain your tabletop as it is.

   ○ Explore it and expand your pile on the table.

   ○ Deny it and attempt to maintain your tabletop.

Anything that happens to you that does not come from your tabletop comes from somewhere else in the room. When your world is "invaded" by something from outside it, you can accept, explore, or pursue it. In those actions, you are saying, "This is real; I will deal with it." When you ignore, deny, or avoid it, you are saying, "This is not real; I'll stick with the reality I know."

Headlines speak of civil wars and massacres: "The streets are running with blood . . . Seventy bodies an hour are floating by in the river . . ." What do we do with such a story? Do we have a place for it on our tabletop, in our worldview? Or do we attempt to protect ourselves from the ghastly inhumanity of the story? Closer to home, imagine losing your child to cancer, or losing your own life years before you expected. Have you made room for this possibility? Our acceptance of, or adjustment to, loss is related to our ability to accept it as part of our world. When we adapt our worldview to include a tragedy, we are better able to deal with its devastating reality.

The same tabletop thinking applies to joy, happiness, and success. They test our worldview too. Perhaps it's the child who wins a scholarship, or the unbounded joy a friend is experiencing over a new love. What do you embrace? What do you withhold from yourself? And what does that say about what you have piled on your metaphoric tabletop?

A positive example from the workplace is that of Muriel, a salesperson in a retail store who would not apply for a management position. When she was encouraged to do so, she replied that she was a salesperson and the company would never promote her to a managerial position. No amount of coaching would change her mind. The possibility of promotion was not on Muriel's tabletop, and this blocked her pursuit of management positions. She worked hard and well, but not to be promoted. One day, some people who worked with Muriel sponsored her candidacy and she was selected for a management job. Now she has added to her worldview the possibility that others can see the skills she knows she has. Look for the Muriel in you and return to the tabletop.

7. Picture yourself sitting in the midst of this mound of stuff on your table, holding up various items and asking what they have to do with each other. Something else falls onto your table. You pick it up and look for its meaning in relation to what you have already accumulated. Look at all that is on your table:

   o How is everything related?
   o What could be the meaning of all of this, taken together?
   o What, if anything, holds it all together?
   o If there were a larger design behind all of this, what might it be?

   Write about these questions.

8. Return to the room that contains the table for a last set of questions:

   o Does the room have doors?
   o If so, where do they lead?
   o Are there other rooms?
   o If so, are they connected?

o If they exist, how would you describe them?

o Together, what might they form?

o And while you are visualizing all of this—your largest vision—where are you as you are seeing this?

The tabletop metaphor suggests a stance toward our lives in the world. It is an acquisitive stance in search of expanding knowledge and experience. It is a proactive stance that leans toward the future and greets new information as friendly. It is an adaptive stance—always learning (another gerund), never fully learned. It is open to imagining the room around the table, to getting the entire room onto the table. It acknowledges the depth and mystery of what is not known.

What can you learn and use from the tabletop exercise? Here are five possibilities:

1. Expand the contents of the tabletop.
2. Open yourself to what else might be out there in the room.
3. Find relationships among the things you have collected.
4. Work with what you are given.
5. Imagine the grand design in which all this makes sense.

Many of us are not conscious that we are building mental structures about how the world really works, but we are doing it nevertheless. Our consistent actions, our habits, our attitudes, and our plans all demonstrate that each of us holds an image or intuition about what the world has done and will do to us. We rely on that image or structure or mental framework to navigate through our world. Without it, we would not know what to do. With it, we often know what to do next. Though we cannot always understand the world, we can build a mental model that explains it to us. The word *model* may not fit your thinking, but thinking in models is useful. Creating a working world model in our head is a useful activity for us when we are exploring our signature path. And, as these pages testify, that model needs to be built from all we have learned and to adapt to what we are still learning. Think of the word *model* in its gerund form, *modeling*, and you are closer to its dynamic nature.

When life experiences come along that do not fit with our understanding of how the world and life work, we have a choice. On the path we take most often, we attempt to force new experiences to fit into our present understanding of how the world works. The other choice is to quit forcing and learn from our most recent experience, which may not seem to fit at the moment.

The second choice is more complex and therefore less likely to be selected. Letting go of our old life model without knowing how we are going to replace it is a brave step. It is even harder to make this decision when we are surrounded by others who are eager to have us do things their way. We need to remind ourselves that what we have recently experienced is real, whether or not it fits with our explanations for life.

CHAPTER NINE

Making Sense
of the World

WE SPEND OUR ENTIRE LIVES FIGURING OUT the world around us and developing mental models of it that allow us to move through it with more joy and less pain. Each day is filled with choices that are based on how we see the world. As you may have noticed, this is a lot of work! It is nice if occasionally others do some of the work for us. Rather than starting from scratch, we can build on what they have done. We turn to the guidance of others when we want to learn more quickly than our limited experience permits.

We are often drawn toward simpler explanations. We want uncomplicated guidance that tells us: "Do this," "Don't do that," "Take these five easy steps to . . . ," "Remember this," "The formula is . . ." In reply, we can say, "I understand; I now know what to do." And we can feel grateful. Our simpler selves want to follow a life path that is cleared and paved. This is easier than choosing and clearing a path for ourselves. We are surrounded by insistent voices offering us easier ways. In addition, many of us have become impatient with how complicated the world has become. Our government, our educational system, our corporations, and our social services seem too complex. Our simpler selves want a world we can understand.

This chapter is a caution sign beside your path: the world often is not as simple as we wish it to be. Be careful with your natural need to make things simple and clear; you can overdo it. You can end up forcing your frameworks, models, or structures onto a twisting, squirming, resisting world. Be cautious in those moments at work when you know what should be done next, when it is simple—and your co-workers seem to refuse to understand and act. Take heed when others are saying, "It is just not that simple."

Don't become entranced with your way of seeing the world and your need for others to see it that way too. And be cautious around others who see the world through boxes, grids, types, styles, and issues. Each of these is a framework or a collection of frames, which can be very useful but can also be overused. Here are some examples:

o Work planning systems that sort people and their performance into a set number of levels

o Instruments that sort people out by their aptitudes or type or personality

o Leadership models that assess people and categorize them by strengths and weaknesses

o Diagnostic questionnaires that sort children by the different ways they learn

o Single-issue people who sort the world into those in favor and those opposed

Nothing is inherently wrong with systems, instruments, models, questionnaires, or issues. They may be very useful structures for helping people understand each other better. The caution is in how we use them. When they become the only lens we use to see and filter the world, their usefulness has been abused. When they become the "truth," rather than the guide, we have reason for concern. When people are told where they fit in a structure, rather than being asked to consider how the structure might fit them, the structure is being abused. In extreme cases, individuals are shoved through simplifying frameworks that sort them into boxes. The illusion is that we now know who those people are and what to do with them. The truth is that complex individuals have been reluctantly sorted into boxes and they are already climbing the walls, cutting holes, and otherwise being themselves.

Given our need to have simple, useful structures to understand the world, and the risk of misusing them, what might we do?

○ Expect complexity. Expect the world to be confusing and fluid. That's the reality; attempt to understand it. Your challenge is to absorb it, embrace it, and not deny it.

○ Seek simplicity. Find the world's meaning in relation to who you are so far. Know that the ways you understand the world are temporary and useful, and that they will continue to change.

○ Look behind the headline. There is a story behind the headline. Find out what that story is. It is the story that displays the richness of life, not the headline. When the headline, the model, the framework is represented as all you need, proceed with caution.

○ Clarify what you believe so far. Do this for yourself and for others. Sort what you know from what you believe. Sort fact from opinion. Sort what you say from what you do, what you think from what you feel. Give time to understanding yourself; this will help others to understand you.

○ Express yourself conditionally. For example, say, "At this time, I'm inclined to think . . ." or "I know I still have much to learn about this, but right now I think . . ." or "Though my thoughts on this might change, . . ." Let yourself and others know the conditions that surround your statements.

○ Notice when you think that you finally understand, or when you believe that you have the correct way of seeing the world. Knowing that you are right blocks your need to continue to learn. You risk moving from being curious to becoming dogmatic and righteous.

Reality's insuppressible complexity counters our quest for simplicity. And reality will have its way, as witnessed by statements like these, flowing from mouths like ours: "This place is a disaster!" "How screwed up can one company be?" "What they are doing is *crazy!!*" We often talk about the world as if it, or some part of it, is a mess. Because we see it as so messy, many of us try to tidy it up and pull it back under our control. Notice how often this doesn't work. And no wonder! We arrived on Earth how many years ago? on a planet that has been here how many billions of years? And *we* are going to straighten it out?

It does sound ridiculous when put in those terms. Many of our efforts are small in relation to the forces we are countering—natural forces, cultural forces, archetypal forces, mythical forces. A wiser and more useful path is to understand more about the world as it is, whether in its more raw and natural forms, like storms or the ocean, or in more adapted human forms, like communities or governmental agencies or grocery stores or major league teams. The world is not crying out for someone to control it; *we* are crying out for control.

The world has an order of its own, a "mind" of its own. We have the opportunity to appreciate it with awe and wonder. When we open ourselves to learning about the nature of the planet and the people on it and their lives and their work, our discoveries multiply. Options are revealed to us that move far beyond those contained within narrower, more controlling perspectives. Plans that do not honor the mysterious, unknowable order of life are doomed to extreme effort, frustration, and probably failure.

Think of family chore allocation systems, think of organizational information systems, think of government social programs, think of all those efforts that didn't work as planned. When you ask the experts why the plans they made didn't work, the response is often "It's a great approach if people will just use it the right way." Perhaps these experts didn't consider deeply enough the nature of the people who were to use the plans.

As John Cowan notes in every issue of his newsletter: "In thirty-five years of working with diesel mechanics, judges, janitors, engineers, salespeople, brokers, teachers, food inspectors, federal bureaucrats, computer-fixers, bankers, factory workers, software developers, and executives of all sizes and stripes, I am delighted to report that: The approach that is based on the fact that people are human is usually the most efficient, the most effective, and the most profitable. The approach that focuses on being efficient, effective and profitable usually stumbles over the fact that people are human."[1] Perhaps this world has an order to it that the experts do not appreciate, that we don't fully appreciate. All of our attempts to understand the world fall short of completion. Just when we think we've got our arms around it, just when we think we comprehend—*wham!* Something comes along and calls into question the order we were creating.

At Sea

We are going to sea for about twenty minutes to help you think about your life in this huge, changing, chaotic world we have been discussing:

EXERCISE

1. Imagine a sailor at the helm of a small sailboat in a large sea. The sailor must use the powers of the sea, the air, and the boat to survive.

2. On a journal page, draw a sailor in a sailboat on that large sea. Provide lots of space in, on, and around the boat for writing. A simple representation of the sailor, the sailboat, and the sea will work.

3. Look at this simple drawing as a metaphor for your life in this world. To your drawing, add lines, sails, wind, rudders, weather, tools, equipment, boats, creatures, people, engines, stars, planets, anchors, clothing—anything that will help this drawing become like your life as it is. If drawing objects doesn't work for you, write words and symbols around the boat that indicate what the sailor is dealing with at sea that is like your

---

1. John Cowan, *Small Decencies,* JohnEdie@aol.com.

life. Or just write a paragraph describing what the sailor faces. Whichever approach you take, spend at least five minutes on the task. Avoid slipping into descriptions of your real life. Stick with the metaphor: What would this sailor face at sea that would be similar to what you face?

4. Finish your drawing or description and step back and look at it. Ask these questions:
   ○ How would you describe the dynamic forces in the drawing?
   ○ Where is the sailboat going?
   ○ How will it get there? What are the primary forces the boat and sailor deal with?
   ○ What are the main feelings conveyed by the picture?
   ○ What, if anything, would you suggest that the sailor do?
   ○ How do you want to change the drawing?

5. Put the drawing aside (overnight, if you can); then return to it and ask the questions in step 4 again. Add to your drawing or description.

6. Consider showing your work to other people who care about the direction of your life. If you choose to do that, give them this chapter and these instructions so they know what you are doing. You could suggest that they complete their own drawing; then you could compare what each of you has drawn. In any case, talk with them about your drawing, or show them your written description.

7. Based on the thinking you've done and the feelings you've had, consider what you've learned through this exercise and ask yourself the following questions. Write your answers in your journal.
   ○ What are the main points you wish to make about your life in this world?
   ○ Where are you going in your life?
   ○ How will you get there?
   ○ What are the primary feelings you have about your life?
   ○ What do you need to do?
   ○ How do you want to change your life?

Moving you temporarily out of your world and putting you at sea may have shaken loose some new ideas or feelings, perhaps something worth further consideration. Metaphors, like sailboats and seas, are life models too. You are fitting yourself into the sailor and the boat the same way you fitted yourself into quadrants and columns earlier in the book. This is all designed to stimulate new perspectives on your path.

Being at sea puts us at the mercy of the forces of nature. We do not argue about whether the high seas are real; we quickly accept it and try to figure out how to adapt to it. This same openness to reality is required in the threatening circumstances of daily life. Accepting what we are seeing or hearing as real may not be as easy in the home or office as at sea. When we are called upon to face the storms that come our way, acceptance is often not our first response. We may attempt to deal with the storm by denying its existence (as in "It may be a problem for you, but it's not for me") or holding to our original course ("I told you weeks ago what I was going to do; nothing has changed"). Or we may give up our control of the tiller ("Do whatever you want; I don't care!").

What do you do when you discover that your self-image is radically different from the way you are seen by some others? What do you do when your best friend breaks a promise? when your honest child has been lying to you? These examples present us with two "truths" that do not fit with each other, for example, "My son always tells the truth. But he lied about where he was last night." A small important part of your world isn't working, and you are faced with a dilemma. A common resolution is to pick one truth or the other and live with the consequences of the choice. Another path involves trying to accept both sides of the dilemma and seeing what comes from doing that.

EXERCISE

Dilemmas

When you are faced with challenges to your present understanding of some part of your life, try this process. We will use the recent experience of my client, Bill, to demonstrate the process:

1. Clearly express the dilemma or contradiction, for example, "I *know* I am succeeding in this work, *and* my boss tells me

I am failing" or "I *know* I am in good shape, *and* my doctor says I have a heart condition." Bill's example is "I *know* that I work well with my business partner, *and* he says that he wants to quit working with me."

Notice that the first statement is yours, is in the present tense, and starts with "I *know.*" The second statement begins with *and*; it states what you have heard from the others. Write each statement simply and accurately. Make the two sides of the issue separate and clear. Use the format "I *know* _____, *and* _____."

2. Look at each half of the dilemma and ask, "How could this be true?" Resist any inclination to make one half of the dilemma true and the other false. Create an explanation in which each half has its own truth. For example, Bill asked, "How could it be true that I work well with my partner? What supports that as truth?" He noted his answers. Then he asked, "How could it be true that my partner wants to quit working with me?" Again, he noted his answers. Seeking the truth of both sides of the dilemma required Bill to open himself to views that were different from his own, allowing the possibility of greater understanding. Do the same with your dilemma: explain the possible truth of each side of the dilemma. The truths for one side may conflict with those for the other side. This is to be expected. List the two sets of truths separately. When you finish, you will have the two statements and a list of supporting truths under each.

3. Put the two statements with their lists side by side. Look at them. Here they are, two separate views of the world that conflict with each other. Each of them makes sense and each excludes the other. If one is true, then the other one isn't— at least that is the way the reasoning often goes.

4. It is time to attempt a leap to another possibility: How could both lists be true? From the higher viewpoint of the reflective self, what allows both lists to be true simultaneously? As Bill considered his dilemma, he found some additional truth possibilities:

a. I am right in my perception of our relationship but something personal is blocking my partner from working with me right now.

b. I was right in my perception of our relationship but something I don't know about has changed it recently.

c. I have always assumed that we had a good relationship. I have never tested that. I have no evidence from him that this is true.

d. My partner wants to leave our relationship for reasons that have nothing to do with me. He has not yet told me the real reasons he wants out.

Each alternative is a possible explanation for both sides of Bill's dilemma being true. Taking this step is a major one: it could help Bill to escape his dilemma, but it also makes him vulnerable. Two alternatives, b and c, suggest that what Bill *knows* about his relationship with his partner is a narrower truth confined to himself.

Back to your dilemma. Develop a short list of possible explanations that allow both sides of your dilemma to be true simultaneously. Open yourself to any alternatives that might explain both sides of the dilemma at once. If you approach this intending to emerge unscathed, you have limited both the alternatives that can be generated and the likelihood of resolution.

5. Test all the work you have done so far with others involved in the dilemma. How might they express the dilemma? What might they list as the truths supporting each side? What explanations would allow everything to be true? As you try to clarify the dilemma together, it will begin to change. Perhaps it will become clearer, or perhaps the emotions behind it will emerge. In any case, you will hear views different from your own.

Bill's partner agreed that they did have an issue and that Bill's statement of the dilemma, the supporting truths, and the alternatives was well expressed. The hard part for both of them was the truth that was revealed. As Bill's partner put it, "You've seen our relationship as a good one, and I do want to quit working with you." When Bill asked his partner about the alternatives, the partner replied. "Your alternative c is most accurate: you've always been wrong about our relationship. You made invalid assumptions, and I implicitly supported those assumptions by not being honest with you. I've always been troubled about how we work together and I haven't told you that, despite having opportunities. I feel awful about that because my hidden feelings are the reason I'm now leaving." By testing his alternative explanations on his partner, Bill got a much better understanding of what was going on. It was still a painful outcome and separation, but Bill now knows that he was only partly responsible.

To deal with your dilemma, consider whom you might test the dilemma, supporting truths, and alternatives on. Think about how you might engage them; consider the possible outcomes for you and whether you are ready to face them. All of this is harder to do when a part of your world is shattered by loss or diminution. Working through these steps does not necessarily result in comfort, but it can yield new thinking, new alternatives, and an awareness of larger perspectives.

Behind all of this lurk the larger perspectives on life that are reflected in the earlier chapters of this book. The world is revealing itself to us; we are creating our own views of it. New views open our options and alternatives. Even as we are imposing our structures on the world, we need to honor its larger, often mysterious, design. In this view, we are constantly learning and refining our notions of what works in the world.

CHAPTER TEN

Yourself and Community

SHEILA KELLY WRITES ABOUT "a sense of place."[1] Sheila writes about the groundedness, the centeredness, that comes with staying put, with settling into a place and a community. I write about change and movement and the individual. I can sense the complementary soul and spirit of our writing that mirrors our marriage. Her words remind me of what I can take for granted, namely, the harbor, the haven, the home that enables me to step forth with confidence—or blocks my stepping forth. Her words remind me to recognize the importance of the people in the many communities we are part of.

---

1. Fritz Hull (ed.), *Earth and Spirit* (New York: Continuum Press, 1993), p. 106.

Think of the communities you belong to, "communities" meaning any group that can define boundaries and purposes that sort it from the rest of the world. What geographic, genetic, political, ecological, professional, social, religious, educational, family, financial, athletic, and electronic communities have your membership? With this wide perspective, you could probably find hundreds of communities that identify you as one of them. You bring different aspects of your self to each community; you

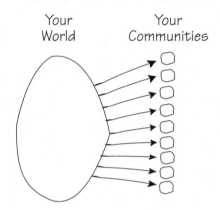

Your World

Your Communities

are the same person, playing different roles. Why do we keep connecting with these groups? What do we hope will happen? How do we declare our uniqueness while becoming one of the many? These are some of the questions we visit in this chapter.

Our engagement with the larger world could be defined by three types of communities: those we choose to become members of, those that define us as members, and those we simply are members of. For example, you probably chose to work for your present employer, making yourself a member of that community. But you may have been surprised when you received a recent bill and found out that you are "part of the family" as far as your favorite clothing retailer is concerned; the store defines you as a member. Add to this the communities you cannot practically choose to leave, like your family of origin and your high school graduating class. Look at the communities in your life through these three categories. Why are you in your communities? What intention is behind your membership? What difference does this make in your participation?

Identity in Community

1. In your journal, list at least eight communities you are a part of. An earlier paragraph offers examples. Select one that is particularly important to you.

2. Write five statements that energetically express how you wish to be seen in that community. Start each statement with "I want to be seen as . . . !" End each statement with an exclamation point.

3. Deliver your statements aloud to yourself with enthusiasm, preferably in front of a mirror.

4. Notice the effect of these first three steps on you. What additional clarity, if any, do you have about how you wish to be seen? What feelings are evoked when you express this to yourself?

5. Select a second, quite different, community and repeat steps 1 through 4.

6. Do the same with a third community.

7. Notice how your statements vary as you move from community to community. Lay out all of your statements about these three communities and see how your expectations differ and overlap. Notice how your different roles affect your expectations and vice versa.

8. What attractions do these three communities have in common? What common struggles do you face across all three communities? Note your answers in your journal.

9. Look back to the eight communities you listed earlier. How did you become a member of each? Did you choose it? Did it choose you? Did you have any choice? What difference does choice make in your investment in a community? Note your thoughts.

The exercise helped you to think about the many communities you participate in. Sort out some that are more important to you and consider why they are important to you. This fits with the book's intention to have you consider your place in the world.

We are looking at your world, then your communities, and then your roles. Each of those roles has a path that intertwines with

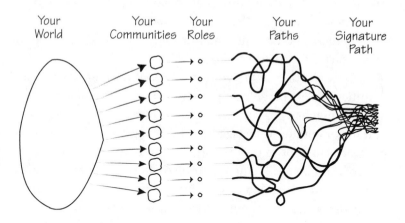

others, forming your signature path, as shown in the illustration.

The line that separates you from others is blurry. Your public self may be observable and relatively clear, but your private and reflective selves are engaged in an ongoing discussion about your identity, about who in the world you think you are, about what you can offer to the world and what you want from it. Your world can be seen through expressions of selfishness and self-lessness. For example, put on your most selfish attitude and read the following paragraph.

"Living with others is a dilemma. There is so much you can get from them—attention, ideas, resources, experience, money, opportunities, happiness, connection, love, technology, guid-ance, goods, services. But to get all that good treatment, you have to be accepted by them and become a part of them. And they might want things from you in return. They expect you to do your share, and they often give you what they think you deserve rather than what you want."

Now, put on your most selfless attitude and read the fol-lowing paragraph.

"Living with others is a dilemma. So many people in the world are in need. You have much to offer these less fortunate people. Many charitable organizations in your community need your abilities and your energy. But people in need are not always easy to serve. They want things their way, even though they have not been in a position where this can happen. They don't necessarily understand or appreciate the help they receive, and they often don't act the way you hoped they would."

Compare these two statements to your position in the communities you are part of. Do you struggle over how much to give and how much to get from each one? Our feelings about our communities range from engagement in giving to pride of accomplishment to guilt to disinterest. Our thoughts range from criticism of those in need to praise for their efforts in adversity. Much of the time, we don't think about this; we just stay busy. We retreat to smaller, accepting communities that reinforce whatever gives us comfort. The smaller the communities we identify with, the greater the possibility that we are hiding out from the larger, more diverse world. In these small enclaves, our consciences can nap and avoid questions like "What do I want from the world?" "What do I want to contribute to it?" and "Who am I in relation to others?" The Commitment Grid attempts to display this.

Commitment Grid

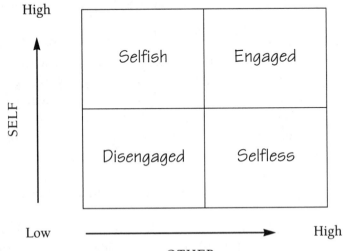

You can see that the individual-community dynamic is alive in this grid. In the upper-left corner (Selfish), we see others as in service to our own needs and we take from them. In the lower-right corner (Selfless), we lose ourselves in giving to others. In the lower-left corner (Disengaged), we are lacking awareness of and commitment to self or others. And the upper-right corner (Engaged) is the "both-and" corner that provides for high investment in ourselves and others.

Human growth is about building values and skills in the Engaged corner. When we look at the setbacks in our lives, we will often find that we have run to one of the other three corners. When we look at the successes in our lives, we will often find that we are engaged together with other people. The "ideal" on this grid varies with the situation, but having the perspective and skills to perform in all four quadrants is most desirable. The Engaged corner expresses high attention to both your self and others. That corner would suggest that you are able to . . .

- Know your own views *and* pursue others' views
- Express what you want *and* try to meet others' wants
- Recognize your rules *and* honor others' rules
- Hold your own beliefs *and* respect others' beliefs

This grid has a double-minded aspect that makes it difficult to grasp. Committing to self and others creates a third position: the ability to see and appreciate both sides without choosing either at the moment. In this position, we can hold beliefs *and* suspend them while appreciating others' beliefs. We discussed this in Chapter Five as the role of the reflective self and in Chapter Six, in View Four of the "Four Sweet Views" exercise.

Suspending beliefs does not mean dropping or concealing or forgetting them. Suspended beliefs are not lost; they are just not being acted upon at the moment. Picture yourself physically suspending your beliefs. You may see that you are still holding them, but off to the side and out of the way of others' beliefs. You can bring them back to your center whenever you choose. If you do change your beliefs, it is because you have chosen to. That's what learning is about.

EXERCISE

Community Commitment

This exercise closes this chapter with a look at your life from the point of view of your reflective self:

1. Draw the Commitment Grid in your journal.

2. Return to your notes from the last exercise, "Identity in Community," particularly what you wrote about your three communities: what you want from them, what attracted you, and what your struggles are.

3. Compare these notes to the Commitment Grid. If you were to roughly sort your statements, one by one, into each of the four quadrants, how would they be distributed? Indicate this distribution by dividing 100 points among the four quadrants.

4. Does this distribution tell you anything about yourself? How does it reinforce or question what you know about yourself? Make notes on this.

5. Think about your life and the many communities you are involved in. Where would you put yourself on the grid? What is your normal, day-to-day stance toward yourself and others? Put a plus sign there.

6. In moments of stress with life or when you have problems with others, where do you move to on the grid? Put a minus sign there. Draw an arrow from your plus sign, where you usually stand, to your minus sign, where you stand under stress.

7. Apart from where you are normally and where you are under adversity, where would you like to be? Mark this third spot on the grid with a star, indicating that this is where you wish to be.

8. Look at what you have just done. Does it represent you well? How does your distribution of 100 points fit with your plus, minus, and star? What would you say about what you have put on this grid? Write this in your journal.

9. Meet with someone you trust who knows you well. Draw a blank Commitment Grid for that person and explain it to

him or her. Ask where this person sees you as operating normally and under adversity, and where you aspire to be.

10. Show the other person your grid. Together, discuss the reasons behind what each of you marked. Talk with this person about your behaviors and what she or he sees you as doing. You might find it useful to place this person on the grid too; then you could talk about your different approaches to dealing with considerations of self and others.

Like most of this book, this chapter is short on right answers and long on exploration and awareness. It helps you to see yourself in relation to others, in the belief that your increased awareness will affect what you do in the communities you're part of.

CHAPTER ELEVEN

The Roles You Play

EXPECTATIONS COME TO US from society, others, and ourselves. These expectations cluster and provide the outlines of the several roles we perform in our several communities. We participate in determining the size and fabric of our roles as parent, member, driver, worker, child, lover, professional, counselor, consumer, learner, friend. As people see us performing in a particular role, they identify us with it. We become the role we are performing, and others "know" who we are by what we do. We "know" what a parent is supposed to do, though the duties we each might include can be quite different. At work, we "know" what we are supposed to do, what the president is supposed to do, and what the salesperson or systems analyst is supposed to do, and they each know what we are supposed to do. Though we may see the same role differently, we speak as if, and may believe that, our expectations are shared.

Our talk about roles usually focuses on how a role should be performed. The voices of experience who pass the role to the inexperienced talk about what to do and when, how to dress and look, what to say and not to say. The reasons behind these Hows are often neglected or assumed to be self-evident. Remember your childhood, or your children's childhood, or taking over an established job, or the role agreements between you and your spouse. Discussions of how things were to be done were the priority. Discussions of why they were to be done were secondary, often emerging from frustrated discussions of the Hows, especially with established roles. Our long experience with how a role is to be performed seems to increase the significance we assign to the Hows and to reduce the likelihood that we will seriously consider the Whys. Recall from Chapter Two the relation of Hows and Whys to what you do. We are revisiting that thinking here as we consider all the roles that the world is ready for us to slip into—whether we are ready or not. The Whys come into play when we take on a role because the reasons behind the role are what shape it to us.

Let's be less abstract. Take the role of parent. A parent who has not thought about or been educated in the Whys of the parenting role is missing a vital perspective. A parent can buy clothing and tools and the books that explain how to perform the role, but he or she will use all those parenting accessories quite differently with the supporting Whys than without. The same can be said of workers, lovers, consumers, and friends and, yes, even systems analysts, secretaries, and salespeople. Without understanding and embracing the Whys, we perform our roles mechanically, haphazardly. An exaggerated emphasis on the Hows results in thoughtless, sporadic, machinelike performance.

Our current personal, work, and community malaise is fed by the absence of Whys in our lives. They are there but we are not encouraged to think about them. We truly do not have time; our time is consumed by the Hows. We have set it up that way, or we are complicit in setting it up that way. We create more and more work with less and less considered meaning. It is not that the work itself is meaningless, but we create work without breathing meaning into it. We invest it with methods, procedures, controls, and consequences, and we leave out the Whys. We are missing Whys in our schools, our corporations, our legal systems, our marriages, our communities, and even our religions, though they were created to deal with the Big Whys. And when we can detect the Whys behind the Hows, we often don't like them.

Whys are always present, whether we address them or not. We can find our own Whys, our own reasons for doing and being. In fact, regardless of what our corporate, governmental, and social institutions come up with, we still have to produce Whys of our own. We cannot help it. We have few ways to escape our Whys. Drugs, credit cards, and compulsive overwork are only temporarily helpful. In the end, we must ask again, "Why is this important to me?"

What can we do about the Whys in our lives? What can we do in this family, this job, this community, starting today? What do we do when we find ourselves struggling within roles that don't fit? Before answering, try this exercise:

Role Survey

1. With your journal in hand, think of roles you currently perform out of choice or by assignment from others. List six to ten of them. If you're stuck, look at the list in the first paragraph of this chapter.

2. Think about each one of your roles for one minute. Visualize yourself performing the role and the duties that come with it. Then move on to the next role until you have thought about each of the roles on your list.

3. Now that you have thought about the entire list, notice the feelings that remain with you. Notice feelings of being overwhelmed or excited, anxious or centered. Briefly describe the feelings in your journal. Notice which roles are more and less attractive to you. Mark them with pluses and minuses. Write down any additional thoughts stimulated by thinking about these roles.

4. Look back over the list again. Underline the roles you chose for yourself. How do you feel about these roles? Note your feelings with a word or two beside each one.

5. Now look at the roles that are not underlined. Beside each one, write who assigned it to you: your parents, your employer, your spouse, your community, our society, or others. Note your feelings about each of these roles.

6. Looking back over the whole list, what would you say about your commitment or lack of commitment to the various roles? How is that commitment affected by what the role is and where it came from? Again, write down any thoughts.

The notes you collected in this exercise provide a backdrop for further elaborations on what our roles can mean. A role frequently has a number of related words hanging on it—*responsibility, expectation, duty,* and *commitment,* to name a few. With these words, the role becomes very heavy. You probably expressed some of that heaviness in the notes you made above. You've certainly found some roles weighty to wear.

You are not your role. You are more. You perform in this one role, you perform many other roles as well, and you are much bigger than all of them combined. Read these three phrases again. You may need to remind yourself of this, or you may not believe it. You are more than the combination of all the roles you fill each day of your life. Each role represents something you have chosen to do with a part of your life. It is possible that you will perform within each of them, but you will *be* none of them.

You are the person behind the roles. You are among the people being served by these roles—the first among many. When this is not true, you've got problems! It happens to all of us, especially nowadays when more roles are possible and each one seems to have a longer "to-do" list. All of this makes it easier to lose your self, your person, behind your roles. If you have any doubt, go to the self-help, business, or parenting section of your local bookseller.

Choose your roles when you can. Life says that many roles will be thrust upon you and you will have to deal with others' expectations of you in those roles. You may or may not meet those expectations, but you will have to deal with them. The roles of son and daughter come to mind. You can shape how you behave as a son or daughter; you cannot decide whether you are going to be one.

Approach each role *as if* you had a choice about being in it. Temporarily relieve yourself of the burdens of being in the role and look at the role from the outside. What would a neutral third party tell you the potential of this role is? What reactions does this role call forth from you? How might those reactions be different for someone else who was stepping into the same role? Think of the stories you have listened to (or the tales you have told) about being the adult child of a particularly difficult parent. Think of lifetimes invested in struggling with an assigned role or against stereotypes. How can you get through such struggles? Try to see imposed roles in a way that empowers you, that enables choice. A role accepted without these considerations often causes us to focus entirely on the power of others over us as victims of a cruel world.

Shape your roles; you often can. Look at the tasks that come with a new role at work. When you are assigned a role, pay attention to the expectations others are sending your way and learn about the role they expect you to perform. Decide if and how you will perform it. The signals that come with an assigned role seem to indicate that you can do little but fit within it, but you usually have more room for self-expression within the role than you imagine at first. Understand the role so you can shape it.

This role has meaning; find it! Start with the assumption that the role is meaningful rather than meaningless. A depressive, burdensome role moves us onto a negative emotional track that blocks exploration of creative alternatives. When you are faced with that knowledge, try on this perspective: many people in the world could step into this role and find great meaning in it. They would be delighted to do what you now dread doing! Where you lack energy, they would be energized. Where you avoid, they would confront. Where you dread, they would anticipate. Imagine yourself looking at your role from their perspective. What would they like about it? What would excite them or energize them? Now, how could you appropriate a little of that energy?

How could you begin to look at the role differently? How could you find the deeper meaning? Ask the help of a powerful and persistent friend to break you loose from your old notions of what this role means.

Work with what life offers you. This is where you are starting from whether you chose it or not. And where else can you start from but where you are standing in your role on your path right now? You can only move forward from here. This is what you've been given right now; this is what life expects of you. Make your meaning from it.

Institutions create roles; individuals create meaning. An enlightened institution, like a business, can create roles with the needs of individuals in mind. It is wonderful when that happens, but the individuals living in the roles still have to find or create meaning for themselves. Good role or bad, we will decide what meaning it has. We are the meaning makers.

PART THREE

Your
Path

[Have] patience with everything unresolved in your
heart and . . . try to love the questions themselves. . . .
Don't search for the answers, which could not be given
to you now, because you would not be able to live them.
And the point is, to live everything. Live the questions
now. Perhaps . . . you will gradually, without even
noticing it, live your way into the answer.

—RAINER MARIA RILKE

RILKE'S LINES OFFER A SWEET OVERTURE to this last part of the book. Here your self joins with your world to define your path. Here your actions in the world express the self-awareness and alternate world perspectives you have been exploring. This is your self touching your world, living the questions now, living your way "into the answer." As Rilke might say, this is you loving the questions, living everything, creating your unique signature path by walking it.

In Part Two, you explored your world, your communities, and the roles that came with them. In Part Three you will explore the paths that emerge from your many roles, paths that unfurl across the landscape of your life, taking you in many directions simultaneously. Your challenge is to bring all of them together, to somehow make them your signature path. And my challenge is to guide you in doing that.

Work will get special attention as we look at your many paths. Many of us are consumed by work, crowding out the possibility of having more of a life outside of work. Our work has its costs and its benefits and is an essential engagement with the world. Or perhaps it is more like a marriage to the world. What kind of engagement or marriage is this going to be? How will it be special? Will it be productive? Is it for better or worse? for richer or poorer? Will this engagement or marriage to work have love in it? And what will we say about it as it ends? Part Three's chapters bring together words and thoughts that are not usually expressed in the workplace: *passion, intention, compulsion, fear, love, suffering, trust,* and *appreciation.* It is an unusual composition. Listen closely and you will hear Rilke's words playing in the background.

CHAPTER TWELVE

Many Paths
Through Life

BEFORE MOVING TOO FAR and too fast down the work path, we will step up and back to view our whole life. Imagine yourself as a surveyor of your life paths. Imagine hiking to a high viewpoint, allowing yourself to see your many paths emerging from your many roles throughout your life. From this high viewpoint, you can survey where you have been, where you are, and where you are going. But before you begin to do this, I want to offer some guidance, using my life as an example. Travel with me on my paths through the next few paragraphs. Use my thoughts to stimulate what you might want to do with your own life survey. Here we go!

We are looking down at my life from a high vantage point. I see my life roles putting me on many paths, stretching me in many directions. I am scattered, I am pulled apart. My roles cut separate paths across a varied landscape. Looking at them from this high point shows that many are headed in the same direction, maybe even moving toward the same destination. I can see the many roles in my life and their paths: writer, husband, consultant, father, skier, reader, friend, speaker, mentor, learner, hiker. When I look back down the writer path, I can see my writing self at earlier points. When I look at the writing path ahead, it is visible for only few yards before it apparently ends in a thicket just beyond my keyboard.

What is true on this writing path seems to hold true on other paths as well. I see myself on different terrain, at other altitudes, at different grades. Each path seems to emerge from its own community, and each seems related to particular roles. Each seeks its own way, occasionally aware of other paths. The writing path wanders among the other paths, connecting with them. Wherever paths join, I sense their implicit attraction to one another. Sometimes they clash with one another. Each intersection suggests where I have been and where I might be going. Roles and paths for helper, reader, lover, learner, hiker, giver, taker. I walk all these paths and more, and they each lead to a realization of some aspect of my self.

Over the years, my paths seem to be blending, making the individual paths harder to distinguish. Five quite separate paths move closer together, joining in a father-son-family-friend-partner path. Work and family paths intermingle, now together, now apart. My initial reaction to the joining of paths is negative; I like being able to distinguish them. I like that each has its purpose, direction, and pace.

My paths have become fewer, meandering toward each other. As I survey and chart them on a page, they become a map of my life. From this vantage point I can see all the paths and the larger territory—even off to distant lands not yet visited. I can see some ascending and descending patterns in my husband and friend paths that are similar, occurring around the same time in my life. Coincidence? I doubt it. I see my father path fading out, changing, perhaps ending. I see my consultant and writer paths moving in the same direction. They seem to be converging on a distant destination. Their convergence suggests what is happening and will be happening in my life. Surveying my life's paths provokes many thoughts for me.

Surveying Your Life

EXERCISE

1. You will need two facing journal pages to do this, though a sheet of paper about two feet square will work even better. Use something you can fold up and put in your journal. If you are feeling more expansive and creative, cover a wall with paper and get a box of markers or crayons. Or gather a few friends with paper and markers, read this section aloud, and engage them in surveying their life as you survey your own.

2. At the edge of one of your pages, list the paths you find yourself on. The roles you described earlier in your journal will help with this. From the many paths you tread, select three that are important to you and different from each other, and that you would like to think about. Use your journal now to draw or describe these three paths that you are walking. Ask yourself:

   o What is the terrain these paths have moved through and are moving through?

   o What is their direction, grade, altitude, and temperature?

   o What does the path ahead look like, or what might it look like?

   o Where do these paths seem to be going?

   Imagine, describe, or draw what comes to mind. Follow these paths wherever they go. Move on to the next step when you are ready.

3. Notice where your paths separate and join:

   o How often do these paths meet? What happens when they do?

   o Which paths seem to be moving toward each other?

○ Which paths seem to separate themselves from the rest? Where are they going?

○ Are your paths going anywhere together? now? later?

Add to your description or drawing. As you refine your paths, you represent yourself better in the world. This exercise is not about getting the picture right, but about understanding yourself in another way. Allow time for this, especially if you seldom engage in these kinds of thoughts. Not having or taking time to think about our paths is more than just a lament; it is often a symptom of paths not taken.

4. Ask yourself a few questions as you survey what you have described and drawn so far:

○ What is the larger territory that contains all of your paths?

○ From what vantage point are you viewing this territory?

○ What path patterns do you see? You might name the country or lands your paths traverse.

○ Where are you on each of your paths right now?

○ How is your many-pathed self coming together? How is it not coming together?

5. Prepare to put your paths and map aside for now. Elaborate on a few descriptions, draw in a few more details, and fold up the map. Do whatever will make the map understandable to you at some later time. Note on your calendar when you want to study this path map again. Do that now, before moving on.

Path seekers are makers of meaning. Map makers are meaning makers too. You are both, in this exercise and in life. As you step back and survey what you have done, your role as a creator becomes especially evident. All that you drew or described came out of your creative self, acting on the world around you. Your higher reflective self does this, and it can do it better when it has the time and height to survey your life in wide perspective. The map you have made represents your emerging signature path in the world. The meanings of the paths and map are inside you, not on the paper. The paper map stands for the internal work you are doing. You are deciding what is meaningful and what is not. You are defining your paths with their twists and turns, meanderings and merges. This is the process of defining your signature path and determining how you touch and change the world.

Next we will narrow our focus to the well-trodden and familiar paths of work. Before reading further, recall work's place among your various communities and roles and the paths you surveyed.

CHAPTER THIRTEEN

The Work Path

YOU WORK. Most people you know work too. You invest a huge amount of your time and yourself getting ready for work, going to and from work, and talking about what happened during work. Love it or hate it, you are giving it a lot of attention, and I am too. Much of our asking, answering, and avoiding of life's questions takes place at and through work. A friend wryly commented, "Work is not my whole life; it's just where I spend all of my time." He is trying to create a life in what's left over after work.

Before you read any further, at the top of a new journal page write the following phrase: "Work is . . ." Below that incomplete sentence, quickly list from six to ten possible endings. This list should set the tone for what you will be reading in this chapter.

Now that you have developed a few thoughts about work, I will add mine. You can compare and contrast our thoughts as you read the rest of this chapter. Work is . . .

o Focal in our lives
o Potentially life-giving and life-consuming
o Essential to a balanced life, along with love
o Out of balance
o Learning applied
o A contribution to the community
o Essential to growth, accomplishment, and mastery

A quick look at our two sets of completions suggests the importance we each assign to work. Our answers give us a sense of the power of work in our lives. There is no escaping work and no reason to—though wouldn't a leave of absence be nice? As burdensome, as exhausting, as tiresome as it can be, you need work and work needs you. Your work may be throwing your life out of balance, but the absence of work would be even more tortuous. Perhaps not so much work, or not this work, or not for money, but work is key to living with meaning. It feeds our need for growth, contribution, improvement, accomplishment, and power. It allows us to socialize, demonstrate skill, get attention, exercise discipline, and experience mastery. You may have been overdoing it lately, which causes you to react against these possibilities, but that could be exhaustion speaking. The wrong work or work overdone does not satisfy our human needs. Much work is worth doing—it feeds your spirit and soul while it feeds you or your family. I hope you are doing that good work; many people are. If you are not and are denying the possibility, you are narrowing your field of vision when you walk the work path.

All of the above implies a definition of work that is larger than a job and smaller than a life. It suggests that work is not bound by paychecks and time clocks, though it might be found within those organizational constraints. Work, good work, might include weeding a garden, or analyzing a financial statement, or teaching a child, or driving a truck, or serving on a jury, or leading a team, or baking bread, or . . . whatever you now give most of your waking hours to. As with the roles discussed in Chapter Eleven, you likely do work that thousands of people would find fulfilling and rewarding, whether you see it that way or not. The tasks involved in the work, the actions essential to getting it done, are not what determine how meaningful that work is to you. Work's meaning is decided by the worker. *You* breathe the meaning into your work.

Think about people you know who are particularly invested in their work. Why is it important to them? And why is that important? And why is *that* important? What is the meaning they extract from their work path? Why do they apply themselves so diligently? Here are stories about three friends and the meaning they make from their work. The stories illustrate three different attractions to work.

Edward has been successfully consulting to work teams in a Fortune 100 company for ten years. He loves his work and feels lucky to have it. I asked him to describe the most significant work in his life. High on his short list was work he did years ago in an ashram in India. His work there included cleaning rooms, washing dishes, and composting human waste for the gardens. He invested all these chores with meaning; he knew he was contributing to the community.

Contribution is one of the great human reasons for work. In volunteer organizations, in the social services, and in politics, the opportunity to contribute to the larger community draws volunteers. They gain the reward of giving to something larger than themselves, the power of being joined with others in service to a larger cause. People making money through their work are not precluded from this satisfaction. In fact, many of them will tell you that it is not the money that keeps them working. It is the opportunity to contribute to the larger community, and they are fortunate to be paid well for doing so. Chapter Ten helped you to think about yourself and others, selflessness and selfishness. Does the perspective you gained there show you anything about your work as a contribution to the community? What communities benefit and how directly?

Lisa pours herself and her love into her work. She has created and runs a home for teenage girls who are struggling with their place in their family and the world. Lisa is motivated by contribution and learning, but in talking with her, I am most aware of the love and caring she exudes through her work. Imagine being responsible seven days a week for eight young women who are living under one roof while pulling their lives together. Lisa's work requires her to give love and she loves generously. Love is part of that home in ways that are not present in the work that many of us do.

Though many of us do not talk about it, we want to give and receive love through our work too. Love is essential to most good work and is as neglected as it is essential. Because we don't talk about it at work, little is done to see that it flourishes. We become aware of it primarily through its distracting permutations, like office romances. This takes our mind off love in its more pervasive forms as expressed in our relationships to our work and to others. I hope you may know the experience of loving the work you do and the people you work with. Love calls forth a larger and finer energy for working than you can bring to work that is "just a job." We will be talking about love and work much more in coming chapters.

Whenever I ask Rosita about her work, she talks about how much she is learning. I know few people who are as intentional and thoughtful about learning from their work and life. She has repeatedly pursued new work duties because of the learning opportunities they offered, occasionally taking salary cuts in the process. She is one of the happier and more integrated people I know, in large part because of her clarity about the importance of learning in her life. This intention to learn contains an ability to stand back and observe herself; it opens her to others because she wants to learn from them. She deliberately takes on work she does not yet know how to do. She models learning for the people she works with by honoring the apprentice as much as the master.

Learning about ourselves through our work is a need that many of us share with Rosita. Work gives us the opportunity to find out who we are as we figure out how to do it. New skills and perspectives at work mean a more developed self. Think of a few examples from your work where you learned a lot. My bet is that many of these situations included interest, challenge, and the opportunity to develop skills. Some of them also included hurt and avoidance. Help in the form of a coach or mentor or guide was also a likely contributor. You got excited because of what you knew and did *not* know. Work can create opportunities to become yourself more fully. In Chapter Four, you inventoried your needs in reaching one destination on your life path. Look back in your journal for what you packed for reaching your destination; it is likely that the list included learnings. As you look back down your path, can you see your learning patterns feeding your life purposes? Think about how aggressively or passively, intentionally or accidentally, you have pursued learning in your life. Perhaps you have found something else you would like to add to your packing list, some learning you need for the trip. Take a moment to expand your list.

Much of our knowledge, our certainty, and our motivation flows from the untidy, unfinished, learning edges of our lives. We give much more conscious attention to what we are learning than to what we have already learned. Our most exaggerated statements about what we "know" often relate to areas where we are still actively learning. Many of us speak with apparent certainty about topics we know little about. Our need to impress blocks our need to learn. We try to make our raggedy edges look more even than they really are. At least I do!

Many motives for working exist: accomplishment, recognition, power, status, and achievement come to mind. Edward, Lisa, and Rosita offer us a glimpse into the importance of contribution, love, and learning as work motives. The examples they provide are meant to elevate these attractions as possible Whys behind the work you do.

To complete this chapter:

o Think about people you know who are deeply and happily invested in their work. Why is this so? Ask them if you haven't already.

o How does what you have just finished reading relate to what you wrote about the four Whys posed in Chapter Two?

○ Look again at the completions you gave for the statement "Work is . . ." What do your words and thoughts clarify about work's meaning to you?

○ How are contribution, learning, and love expressed in your work life? Provide yourself with examples of each.

○ What have you been learning about work's place on your signature path?

Spend this time thinking and writing in your journal before moving on.

CHAPTER FOURTEEN

Passion
at Work

IVAN IS A SCULPTOR OF METAL. He loves his work; he is passionate about it! He is a huge, powerful man with large hands hard-
ened by years of shaping metal. His voice and his heart are as big
as his hands and they all express his love of this arduous, artful
craft. He works day and night for weeks at a time, shaping and
casting the massive sculptures he is known for. Commissioned
work and gallery sales barely support him and his family. He cannot imagine doing anything else.

One definition of passion is an "intense, driving, or over-
mastering feeling or conviction." How does this definition fit
with your feelings about your own work? What powerful or compelling emotions do you experience in the pursuit of your work?

Another definition is "strong amorous feeling; love." Test that against what you feel at work. The word *passion* comes from the Latin *pati,* to suffer or submit. How does that fit? Notice the feelings passion arouses in us as it pulls on our emotions, or arouses us, or causes us to suffer. All of these definitions together express an array of feelings that can be associated with the passionate path of work—work as powerful emotion, submission, and suffering. These interwoven themes snake along the work path, bringing agony, ecstasy, and meaning.

Sylvia is a CPA and, by her own declaration, she loves the numbers! Her clients stick with her because they know that she is serving a god larger than their annual bill from her. She speaks strongly and lengthily about the importance of solid numbers to a sound business. She will not let her clients or government regulators get away with anything. At tax time, she works seven days a week, ten to sixteen hours a day, to get her clients' books in order. She gets great satisfaction from balancing an account or finding ways to save her clients money. Being a CPA is exciting, life-fulfilling work for Sylvia. It suits her; she intends to keep doing it for at least twenty more years.

Work and passion are seldom considered together. Anger and passion? Yes. Sex and passion? Certainly. Politics and passion? Okay. But work and passion? This chapter searches for the passion we bring to our work, the ways we pursue it, and the ways we express it. It is about the potentially compelling, passionate relationship between work and the worker. We often speak of work as a burden that is laid on us by others, as if we had no choice in taking on the burden. Listen to yourself; listen to others. Listen to Barnie in this example.

Not long after Barnie started downhill skiing, he discovered "the bumps," those vertical fields of hills and holes that experienced skiers, and some dumb skiers, try to slide through upright on narrow boards. Barnie never made it through one of these fields without falling repeatedly, usually hurting himself, but never seriously. After doing this all day, Barnie would join his friends in the bar and tell stories about how he had almost killed himself. Why did Barnie go through all that pain and all those stories? Because he loves to ski, and to learn, and to risk, and to be recognized. No one forces him down those bumps but himself.

This story speaks for many of us, not just for Barnie. We do not need steep, snowy slopes to pursue this kind of passion. We find it in many places and many of us find it in our work. There we can do, learn, suffer, achieve, moan, love, brag, and get rewarded for it! We are clearly getting something from this dedication to work. Something explains the driven behavior of many people today. Passion for work is the explanation we will explore here—not that there aren't other possibilities. To get yourself into this from a new perspective, work through this exercise.

EXERCISE

Passionate Pursuits

1. Recall three pieces of work you dedicated yourself to fully. They could be:

   o Something that you studied or attended to over a long time

   o Something that you really liked to do, that you couldn't keep off your mind

   o Something unique to you—or at least something that most people were not doing

   o Something that made an important difference in your life

2. In your journal, write down each of these pieces of work with a few phrases describing each of them.

3. Why was this work important to you? Write about that.

4. Why is what you just wrote important to you? Write about that.

5. Where is this writing leading you? Write about that. This is a path toward passion in your life.

6. Next, think back through your life to someone you dedicated yourself to fully. This person could be:

   o Someone you dedicated yourself to or attended to over a long time

   o Someone you liked to be with, whom you couldn't keep off your mind

   o Someone special to you and for you

○ Someone who made an important difference in your life

7. In your journal, write down the person's name and a few phrases describing him or her.

8. Why was this person important to you? Write a few phrases about that.

9. Why is what you just wrote important to you? Write about that.

10. Where is this writing leading you? Write about that. This is a path toward passion in your love life.

We want good work and good love, though not necessarily in that order. Look back down your path and see how it has sought good work and good love. We dedicate most of our waking hours to either or both of these. The search for good work means much more than finding a job. Good work engages you, helps you, rewards you, and contributes to others. The search for good love extends beyond romance or sexual satisfaction to relationships that are honest, caring, and fulfilling. We search for work and love infused with learning and excitement and opportunity. See how this paragraph fits with what you wrote a few moments ago. Work and love fill our human hearts and minds with meaning; they are essential to our self-esteem and self-creation. Most descriptions of people's signature paths probably include words like the ones you wrote in the last exercise and I wrote in this paragraph.

We envy people who love their work, as we do those who have successful marriages or relationships. Envy is not the most admirable of human traits, but it certainly points toward something we want for our own lives. We want work and love to be bound up in each other even when the structure of our work and our lives tries to keep them separate. The intentional separation is well expressed by the old company "wisdom" that tells workers to leave their personal lives and problems outside the door when they come to work. Go to a bookstore and look at all the books on work and love; notice that they are not displayed together.

As work structures change, as we move away from the assembly line and time clocks toward home offices and flextime, the separation of work and love, task and relationship, becomes more obviously artificial. People are searching for more meaning in their work and their work relationships, when they have the least time for it. Maybe I am reaching a little too far for some of you. Maybe you aspire to something more, less, or different. But I'd be surprised if your expectations about work were not somehow bound to caring, respect, affection, and love.

Romancing the Grindstone

EXERCISE

Here is an exploration of love and work:

1. Imagine that you are deeply, passionately, in love with someone—perhaps it's the person you wrote about earlier in this chapter. Now imagine that you love this person as you have always wanted to love, and that you are able to express your loving thoughts, feelings, and actions more completely than ever before. Imagine the depth of your feelings and the power of this love relationship. Imagine what you would do with this person, what you would say, how you would express your love, how you would share your time. Try answering some of these questions in your journal:

- How much of your time would you spend with this person in your thoughts?
- What might you say to this person near the beginning of a day together?
- What might you be thinking about the person during the day together?
- What would you say to the person at the end of the day together?
- What would you say to others about this person?

Answering these questions now may feel a bit awkward, but please write down your thoughts. Your thoughts and answers will remind you of the passion you have had, or want to have, in your love life. You know how much of this love you have actually experienced in your life, and you have some sense of how much more you would like to experience. I hope your life has included a generous helping of the love you were just describing. Now put those notes and thoughts aside and move on.

2. Imagine that you have wonderful, compelling, and deeply engaging work. Imagine that this is the work you have always wanted to do. Through it you are able to express your thoughts, feelings, and actions more completely than ever before. Imagine the depth of feeling involved, the power of the work. Imagine what you would do in this work, what you would say, how you would express yourself, how you would give yourself to it. Now, quickly, answer these questions in your journal:

   o How would you feel at the beginning of a day of work?
   o How much of your time would you spend with your work in your thoughts?
   o What might you be thinking during a workday?
   o What would you say about your work at the end of a day?
   o What might you say to others about your work?

   Answering these questions could be a pleasant reminder of the work you have or the work you are searching for. I hope your life has included a generous share of what you were just feeling. What you just thought, felt, and wrote about is your expression of the passion you want to bring to your work.

3. Compare your two sets of answers. The questions differed only in their focus on love or on work. How are your answers to the two sets of questions related? Write a paragraph explaining that relationship.

Consider your underlying passions for work and love. No, they are not the same, and they don't meet exactly the same needs, and they probably don't substitute that well for each other. Experience shows that work is often used to fill in for the absence of love (and vice versa, come to think of it). What is the common prescription for someone who has recently lost a love? Keep busy in your work! It is not unusual for someone without good work to turn to a love relationship to find that missing satisfaction. Think about couples who attempt to combine their love for each other with their love of work by building a business together. These examples reinforce the connection between love and work. The potential passion for each of them is within us; they both are necessary for full human existence. Love and work are not as emotionally separated as they are often portrayed.

We love our work and our work cannot love us back. If it could, it would do a lot more for us:

○ If our work loved us back, it would see to it that we were regularly praised and appreciated. We would hear in elaborate detail about how the finer points of our work are valued.

○ If work were a decent lover, it would give us the recognition we deserve for our accomplishments, without our having to hint around. Work would provide praise, bonuses, promotions, opportunities to grow, professional recognition—and parties.

○ If work loved us right, it would always understand when we took a risk that didn't succeed. Work would lovingly offer us another chance.

○ And work would always recognize us as special people with unique talents, aspirations, issues, and opportunities. Work would never neglect us; our needs would always be paramount.

These are among the many things work would do for us if it could love us back, but it can't. So what we get back, we set up for ourselves or a few generous others provide. Love of work is a one-way love. Our friends can love us back; our work cannot. Too often we pour ourselves into our work as if it should give something back to us from outside ourselves. The rewards of work are largely intrapersonal; we bestow them on ourselves. When we love our work, we are loving a part of ourselves.

Engaging work cuts two ways: as it fulfills us, it also separates us from others who are not a part of it. When we pour ourselves into work, physical, mental, emotional, and spiritual distance is created between us and people who are not working with us. The same can be said of engaging love. Important work and love relationships have consequences for those outside of them.

Recently three overworked managers and I were discussing how to put some boundaries around work. Their workloads were damaging their productivity, their mental health, and their families. All three used the same method for getting a little extra work done in the evening: they would help get the kids to bed, spend a little time alone with their spouse, and then stay up after the spouse went to bed, reading work that had not yet been done that day. This was their pattern. The four of us considered the choice between work and love that possibly was being made here—working into the night versus being in bed with their mate. We didn't talk together about this very long, but we had clearly touched on an important choice. Our choices about work and love often come down to questions like this, and having thought about them makes these choices easier.

Today's chaotic work world supports substituting work for love. The world is pulling apart the old relationships that gave us love—marriage, family, community, church, schools. And the work world is more demanding and less secure than at any time since World War II. You know the story: global competition, information technology, the marketplace, and change. We are streamlined, reengineered, delayered, downsized, and desperate. And yet we are hopeful about work as a path to life meaning. It is likely that you see your work as a piece of your fuller self. And you are probably not reading this at work, but instead are trying to crowd it into an exhausting day. You still perk up at articles and conversations about becoming yourself through powerful work. This idea excites you! You know what it is to love your work, or you know it to be a worthwhile aspiration. Realization of this aspiration could be another matter.

We are privileged to be living in a time when we can talk about this. Billions of people have gone through life seeing work only as a necessity lacking promise and fulfillment. We need to remind ourselves of the special historical circumstances we have inherited at the same time that we aspire to improve on what we have received. It is precious, won by predecessors who worked to lift themselves up, and, in doing so, lifted us up as well.

Many of us love our work—or at least some aspect of it. We pour our passion into our work and have little left to spend outside of it; we are spent. We look to work to meet all of our needs, or we don't do anything but work and so preclude other needs from being met. We make work more important than anything else, we are excited by it, we succeed at it, and we give more and more of ourselves to it, which leaves less and less of ourselves for others.

JOURNAL

Some journal notes would close this chapter well. Ask yourself:

o When you give yourself to work, what do you get back?

o How does work feed or starve the rest of your life?

o What do the important people in your life tell you about your work? How do they say it affects you and them?

o What are you learning in this chapter about love, work, and your passion?

We live in a world that strongly supports overwork. The demands of work leave many of us dissatisfied. Too often we rely on work for more than it can give, and we use it to displace other essential sources of life satisfaction. Your own signature path may be about dealing with the dilemmas that work has created for you. Look where your present path leads. Does it excite you? Does it bring you joy? What do you want to do about it?

CHAPTER FIFTEEN

Paths Not Taken

IN CONSIDERING PASSIONATE WORK as a part of your signature path, you cannot neglect the shadowy sides of passion. Think of a person you have seen acting with passion. Assess that person against these three qualities: perspective, balance, and control. How's the fit? Passion for many of us fits with loss of perspective, loss of balance, and lack of control. This may be why some of us are attracted to passion but are afraid of it. Passions like love, anger, desire, greed, lust, joy, and hate are all strong emotions, compelling feelings. They operate outside the rationality that many of us believe is central to who we are. We suspect excessive emotional enthusiasm; we shy away from extravagant feelings.

When someone is passionate about an idea of mine, or a cause of mine, or me, a disturbing jumble of thoughts and feelings comes forth: "Hold it! This is great, but let's not go overboard." "Wait a minute, aren't you getting a little out of control here?" "Yes, yes, but let's slow down and look at what's really possible here." These are the more rational expressions of fear of loss of perspective. They must be put beside words that come from another part of the self: "Yes! Do it!" "Go for it!" "Follow this feeling!" "Let go and live!" We each get caught in our own version of this dilemma. We each ride a seesaw of life between freedom and control, emotion and rationality. Some of us ride close to the fulcrum; others are frantically flailing away at either end.

"Let go and live!" Ask yourself:

o What are your responses to this exhortation?

o What have you been thinking about while reading this?

o What passionate paths have you taken and not taken?

o What fears and longing are evoked in you?

o What dreams do you keep dreaming and not enacting?

o What reasons do you offer for continuing to do what you are continuing to do?

Take a few minutes to respond to these questions in your journal. Focus especially on the questions that are less comfortable for you. Also notice your reaction to the request that you do some thinking and writing about this.

Alternatively, spend a few minutes thinking about passionate people who have acted in ways you admire:

o What did they do?

o How did they do it?

o What might you learn from them?

o How might you learn it?

Many of us are afraid of our passion for the paths not taken, for the lives we chose not to live. We fear that in acknowledging those other paths, we can unleash forces that will tear up the paths we are on. We protect ourselves from the unbalancing weight or lightness of these passionate extremes. We hold on to what we may call sanity or security or comfort or common sense. And yet we wonder about our unchosen, more passionate paths.

Hide and Seek

EXERCISE

Let's play with the following question: Where do you keep your passions? Imagine your way through these steps and make notes about them in your journal.

1. Imagine that you are going to keep your passions in one place. Imagine that it is possible to put them in a container or on a shelf. Where might you keep them? In the closet? behind a door? on your sleeve? in a bottle? on a mountaintop? on a shelf? in a cave? buried in the sand? in your top desk drawer? Imagine a place that fits for you. Name and describe it in your journal before moving on.

2. Now name the passions you would keep there. Write them all down and think about why each is on the list to be put in this place.

3. Where you choose to keep your passions might tell you something about what you believe they are. For example, passions kept on a mountaintop might be lofty and challenging, or distant and inaccessible. Passions kept behind a door might be closed or opened as you choose. Stop for a moment to consider the place you imagined and what it might mean. List words and phrases you associate with this place.

4. Now that you have described the place where you keep your passions, how do you get to it? How would you reach your passions? Is the place close by? What do you need to get there? How public or private is it? What feelings surround this place? Write a few lines about this.

5. Remember the tabletop you piled with everything from your life, back in Chapter Eight? Think back. Did you include your passions, known and unknown, on that tabletop? Do you have room in your life for this unruly, fervent side of yourself? Look back to that exercise and see what you

described; compare it to what you have written here, and add that information.

6. Your last step has to do with safe access. Given where you keep these passions and how you have described them, what might be some reasonable ways of learning more about them if you choose to? How might you move toward them? How might you bring them to you? Who might you ask to accompany you? What tools or resources might be helpful to you? (Remember your four-box inventory in the Possessions Chart in Chapter Four.) Think about this for a moment. For some of you, this will be a step into pretty squishy ground; for others, it will be a solid step onto the visible path to your future. But squishy or solid, the opportunity exists to open carefully to your unknown, more passionate self.

Here are other aids to making passion an ingredient of your signature path:

o Get a guide to help you in the ascent or descent into your passions. This book is an example. Finding a coach, counselor, mentor, or therapist is also a possibility. Choose somebody who has been there before and who can help you to make the trip. This may involve talk over coffee or many meetings over months, depending on the trip you want to take.

o Read more about what you suspect you are likely to find when you arrive. This book and many others can help. Visit the self-help and business sections in your bookstore.

o Read more about the process of plumbing your deeper self. This could increase your confidence for the trip.

o Talk with good friends about your thoughts. You might have them read this chapter and talk with you about it. The shadowy path toward unknown or unacknowledged passions becomes better lighted in the company of friends.

o If this chapter is at all intriguing to you, then do something about it—something that moves you forward in learning about your mysterious, passionate self.

CHAPTER SIXTEEN

When Your Path
Is Steep

ONE DEFINITION OF PASSION has to do with suffering. Suffering
contains elements of submission, inevitability, and giving yourself over to what is being pressed upon you. This certainly has
something to do with many people's work. We are going to
explore this suffering side of passion for a few pages.

Chance, genetics, ability, hard work, and being born at the
right time have much to do with the good and bad news in our
lives. I hope you are thriving! But even if you are, you know that
life is not easy. You may know suffering on intimate terms. Here
are some reminders of how we suffer:

○ *For failure,* when we invest ourselves in something or someone and it does not work

○ *For others,* when we join in the pain of people we love

○ *For ourselves,* when we hurt as a result of living with our own shortcomings

○ *For fate,* when we are unlucky or in the wrong place at the wrong time

More sources of suffering could easily be found, but this is a start.

JOURNAL

Before balancing this suffering side of yourself with lots of reminders of just how happy and wonderful you are, return to the "Surveying Your Life" exercise in Chapter Twelve. Look out over the life roles and paths you listed there and consider the following questions:

○ How have you suffered in your life?

○ Which life roles caused you to suffer more and less?

○ What patterns do you notice in the sources of your suffering?

○ What patterns do you notice in the way you deal with suffering?

○ How important has suffering been in making you the person you are today?

○ Do you feel inclined to skip this writing about suffering? Why?

The questions are intended to stir your thoughts and feelings. Your answers are less important than the overall inclination you feel to move closer to, or farther from, consideration of suffering in your life. We do not need to bask in suffering, but not seeing it means not learning from it. This is the challenge: How do we suffer and learn from it without being pulled down and paralyzed by it?

EXERCISE

Nathan, Adam, and You

1. Nathan and Adam are executives with different views of suffering. Read about them keeping the following question in mind: What are the positive and negative consequences of these different views?

You may not get as much information as you would like about these two men, but you will have enough to stir your thinking about what the results of suffering less, or suffering more, might be.

2. Nathan leads a life of considerable worldly success. He comes from a strong family background, his twenty-year marriage is solid, and he has recently been promoted to a job he loves. If you ask Nathan about his suffering, he is likely to give you a blank look that says, "What are you talking about?" He will brush off further consideration of the question. Nathan has not suffered much in his life—he has had no major illnesses, accidents, failures, losses, or deaths. The few broken bones and setbacks he has experienced did nothing to dent his shiny, positive self-expression. Nathan sees the world as an exciting opportunity and steps boldly into the fray. He talks and acts as though he were indestructible. Given Nathan's lack of experience with suffering, what other consequences would you guess might be visible in his actions? Note a few of these.

3. Adam also leads a life of considerable worldly success. However, his parents divorced early, his own second marriage is a little rocky at the moment, and though he is in a job that he does quite well, it is not the job he believes he deserves. If you ask Adam about suffering, he is likely to give you a knowing nod that says, "Tell me about it!" He sees himself as suffering a great deal in life. New projects are taken on as new burdens to carry. He carries them well, but heavily. Adam's physical movement seems to reflect the invisible load he is carrying. He moves cautiously into new situations, but he does move into them. He is a smart, successful executive who often wonders aloud whether he will survive the day. Given Adam's experience with suffering, what other consequences would you guess might be visible in his actions? Note a few of these.

4. Nathan's and Adam's experiences with and expectations about suffering are distant from each other; they might represent normal extremes with regard to suffering. Each of

their orientations toward suffering makes sense, given their histories. Their actions are quietly influenced by how they see the likelihood of suffering. Based on the notes you made about each of them, compare and contrast these two men. Use what you have read about them to think about the possible consequences of their orientations. This is not a prediction of what either Nathan or Adam might actually do; instead, it is your thoughts about the possible influence of suffering or the lack of it on their lives. Make notes on the strengths that each might bring to dealing with the issues of their work and lives.

5. Ask yourself these questions:

   ○ How are you like Adam? like Nathan?

   ○ How do you see the world?

   ○ What are the consequences you expect?

   ○ What prophecies are you making for your future?

   ○ How do you go about fulfilling these prophecies?

   Write about these questions, and think of yourself in these terms.

6. An important element of our look into the lives of these two executives is their stance toward the world, how they meet the world, in an almost physical way. How do you meet the world? Are you leaning forward, seeking new experiences, not just receiving them? Are you leaning back, receiving new experiences but not seeking them? These are two of many possible postures toward the world. How do you picture yourself? Where are your feet? Where is your torso? What are your arms and head doing? If you can, move into that physical stance right now. Put yourself in place to deal with the world, ready to handle what comes your way. Imagine yourself as a statue titled "Dealing with the World," with your name on it. We could have you bronzed! Notice the feelings within this statue and write them down.

Here is one interpretation of these two executives to put beside your own: Nathan, through his experience, expects not to be harmed and is blinded to the possibility of suffering and failure. Adam, through his experience, expects to be harmed and is blinded to the possibility of comfort and success. They are each absorbed in what they "know" will come their way. Their views shape their worlds and their actions; they have each ended up receiving what they anticipated. The self-fulfilling prophecy strikes again! Nathan's perspective on the world causes him to see and act upon what reinforces his perspective on the world, and the same is true for Adam.

Through experience and accomplishment, Nathan brings a clear eye for the future and a positive spirit that helps him to see opportunities, which loom larger than the obstacles. He is impatient with those who want to delve into details about how to make the future work and he does not need long discussions of alternatives and obstacles to make decisions. He moves forward quickly. Adam successfully uses his long experience in working in a world where the odds are against him. He anticipates potential problems and figures out how to deal with them before they arrive. He is ready for them. He makes sure he has the support he needs to move ahead by engaging people he can count on. He has his larger goals in mind as he plans how he will deal with each hurdle that could be thrown in his path.

Each of these executives has developed a unique way of walking his signature path, and both of them demonstrate a strong pattern of accomplishment. Their backgrounds have shaped them and they have each learned. They each deal with the world as they see it.

Here's another possible way to view suffering. Over the last two years, my friend Jessica has made it through the establishment of her business. She faced rejection, financial need, loss of confidence, lack of business, and her own ignorance about how to run a small business. In other words, it was a pretty typical and difficult startup. She clearly got more for her pain than gray hairs. She has survived; she thrives! She was tempered in the fire of experience and purified, and her life was altered. She has a new calm and new confidence. This is not to say that everything is working wonderfully. Jessica still faces many of the same trials she had before, but they are easier because of what she has learned. And she will suffer again, but perhaps with more confidence that the process can have rewarding outcomes.

All that Jessica and the rest of us suffer through does not automatically result in wisdom, perspective, and insight. It may just be suffering; we may learn nothing. But the suffering is at least an indication that we might find some opportunity here. Without suffering and submission to what the world is bringing us, the likelihood of fast and significant growth is reduced. When your suffering arrives, look for the learning being offered and remember your stance toward the world. As Viktor Frankl said, "When a man finds that it is his destiny to suffer, he will have to accept his suffering as his task; his single and unique task. . . . His unique opportunity lies in the way in which he bears his burden."[1]

 Read the Frankl quote again:

o Can you think of a time in your life when these words especially applied?

o What was the burden you carried then?

o What was the opportunity for you in bearing that burden?

o What did you learn through the difficulty of the process?

o How might that serve you in the future?

After writing about this, take a break before reading the next chapter.

1. Viktor Frankl, *Man's Search for Meaning* (New York: Washington Square Press, 1984), p. 99.

CHAPTER SEVENTEEN

Your Intentions and Choices

WE LIVE OUR LIVES IN THE OVERLAP between what we intend to do and what we choose to do. Our outside world constantly seems to be asking or telling us to look at our intentions: "Do you really want that?" "You should want this!" That outside world calls for us to adjust to its version of reality, to choose it. This is the world our public self lives in. But we also have an inside world and a private self that wrestles with what we know, feel, and want, and a reflective self that, if it can get a word in, cares about who we are becoming and what we might do to realize our purposes.

Picture these three selves forming a triangle in dynamic balance on the point of the moment. As any one of the three selves shifts, the others are also forced to move to maintain the balance and to keep from slipping off the point. The three selves constantly shift as they adjust to each other and to the point of the moment. And the moment is shifting through time; it is never in the same place.

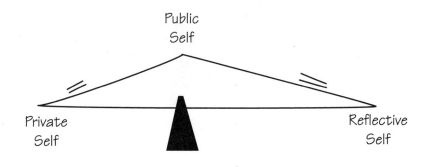

Many of us yearn for more stability than that. A solid balance, nailed to the point of the moment with equilibrium between our three selves, would suit us just fine. In Chapter Nine, we discussed the part of us that wants simple resolution, the answer, the conclusion. But years of "life research" demonstrate that this static resolution cannot be maintained; it slips away, leaving us off balance again. It loses the very qualities that drew us to it: its reliability and the security of knowing the "truth." With this loss and the resulting imbalance, we are left unresolved in a world where certainty seems ephemeral, truth is in turmoil, and our foundations are being undermined. This new reality challenges us to find a new resolution, a new balance—and here we go again.

With the new reality comes new learning that suggests that no new and final balance exists, but a continual balancing. (See the material on gerunds in the introduction to Part Two.) We are constantly weighing intention and reality against each other and we are choosing. Shifting our weight allows progress. We learn from what is happening in this moment and we use it in the next. We anticipate what is coming based on past experience. We become clearer about both what we intend and what exists, allowing subtler dynamics to emerge. And we know that this balancing never ends but is always in process. Our lives are not hanging in the balance. Our lives are the balance and the balancing. Living is balancing.

When we search for the meaning of life, we find it in the process of living. Life is not in the resolution, but the resolving. Not in the answer, but the answering. Not in our decisions, but in the deciding. The resolution, answers, and decisions that occur along the way are markers of movement. They indicate that something happened between where we were then and where we are now. Achievements, birthdays, failures, anniversaries, births, and deaths are markers too. They tell us that we have moved, but they are not the movement. These significant markers stand along our life path. They mark our movement along our signature path, but they are not our lives any more than a road sign on a highway is our journey. We are the travelers; we read the signs and use them in deciding where we have been, where we are, and where we are going.

And all of this has something to do with the following three vignettes. How are these three vignettes related?

1. When Alaskan sled dogs are learning to pull sleds, the lead dog is trained to keep moving, no matter what. In the absence of knowing where to go, the lead dog is to behave as if it knows where it is going. To do less is to create pandemonium as all of the other dogs begin to pull in different directions and to fight with each other.

2. A couple from Buffalo, New York, was curious about the many towns or cities in the United States named Buffalo. They found over thirty and decided to visit each of them. In the process, they found a dozen or so more, visited those Buffaloes too, and wrote a book about the whole trip titled— what? Of course, *Buffalo*. An interviewer once asked them why they had made this pilgrimage to Buffaloes. This is my recollection of their response: "When you come to a fork in the road, it's nice to know which way to turn. We turn toward Buffalo."

3. A unique ability I have had since early in life is that I can always point toward north. Ask me to point north on an elevator, or in a strange city, or in the middle of the night, or

all of the above, and I will do it. Sometimes I have to think about it for a moment, but then I point. I use this ability to get out of buildings or across town or up to mountain lakes. I rely on this talent frequently. It is a great aid to me, though I am often wrong! Many of us men have this talent, which enables us to drive for hours without asking for directions!

The question of the moment is this: What do these three vignettes have to do with each other? Spend a couple of minutes thinking about this and making up answers.

The three stories share the quality of directed, arbitrary movement—choices for the sake of movement, arbitrary destinations for the sake of movement. The movers in these stories know enough about what to do next to keep moving, but they do not know where they are going. The immediate choices they make keep them moving, with the hope that the movement will inform them. This is especially clear with the sled dogs who are moving with no destination. It is also true when I don't know true north even though I intend to go somewhere, and it is true for the Buffalo seekers. Their choice of Buffalo makes no more and no less sense than choosing Peoria or Kingston or Ferndale and they know it. Choosing is what is important. The choice allows them to keep moving and experiencing life along the way, which is their real intention. Other choices that kept them moving would have made as much (or as little) sense. Choosing Buffalo was more important than the choice of Buffalo. Guessing about north is more important than being right. Moving dogs is more important than getting to some specific place.

Please don't confuse this dynamic choosing process with needless busyness. This choosing leads to awareness and excitement as we scan our internal and external surroundings. It's a leaning-forward-in-your-harness awareness with a receptiveness to what you encounter. These examples each have a physical aspect to them that could be pursued single-mindedly, focused entirely on destination rather than on the discoveries that come with an emerging path. Too much destination-focused energy, too narrow an energetic awareness, and you will lead yourself away from allowing the path to work. The path is defined by the movement, and making a choice is often more important than the choices you make.

Consider these questions:

- o Do I know my intentions? Can I choose?
- o What is the difference my choice could make?
- o Is that difference important?
- o What is more important, the choosing or the choice?
- o What best represents progress, intentional movement or a thoughtful decision?
- o Do I know enough about the options to choose between them?
- o When I don't know enough about the options, is my actual choice important?

How might we apply this homemade wisdom to our own lives? Should we train a sled dog? vacation in Buffalo? buy a compass? No—just keep trucking. (If you have been around awhile, you may be seeing a bumper sticker from the seventies hanging on the brown and orange wall of your old hippie mind.) Lean forward in your harness; be intentional about moving into your future, wherever that may be. And choose. Go left or right, in or out, down or up, but choose. Don't make a habit of standing on your signature path. Point to the north and move out, knowing that you will often be wrong. Head toward Buffalo.

CHAPTER EIGHTEEN

Appreciation Deserved

PART OF WHAT MOVES US along our work path is the recognition we receive from people around us. It is not everything, but it is important to most of us. We are social creatures and our lives are profoundly infused with and informed by our communities. Other people are critically important to us; we act with ourselves and them in mind. Each of us carries a private awareness of what we do for the good of the whole. And many of us feel that we do more than we are appreciated for. We work our tails off outside the limelight and feel unrecognized. We take pride in what we do, and in our ability to do it without constantly receiving attention from everyone we are helping. At the same time, many of us are disappointed or resentful or saddened or angered by the lack of gratitude coming our way. We find delicious the memories of the occasions when others expressed their appreciation for our efforts.

This chapter is about being appreciated more for our work. We will think about giving and receiving, attention and neglect. Though the chapter is about work, it takes a personal turn because appreciation is rooted in the heart, not in the performance review. The source of appreciation, combined with our need for it, makes us vulnerable. In need, we become extra-sensitive to what is said about us. Gratitude from important others seldom pours forth by the bucketful. It drips out at unpredictable times. We often hang around hoping to catch an earful, and most of us yearn for more than a drop now and then.

Think about how much of your work you do alone. Nobody around. Just you and your work. You know how diligently and creatively you apply yourself to finishing a project on time, under budget, within specs. You know, but nobody else does because they weren't there. They were busy doing their own hard work and feeling unappreciated by others for doing it. You know the hours you spent analyzing these data, or building this unit, or creating this recommendation, or—you fill in the blank. The work product is better for the care you have taken, the sweat you invested. But the work can't speak for you. The work speaks for itself. It can't say what you would like to have it say. You end up choosing to speak for yourself—or not to speak, hoping that somebody will notice. After all the work you put in, now you are thinking about tooting your own horn to get the recognition you deserve.

During a break in a meeting with a group of friends, one friend privately told me about a major contract she had just signed that was bigger than any her firm had ever signed before. She quietly told me her good news. I was happy for her and quietly told her so. She also told me that she was not mentioning her success to the group because they might see her as bragging or raising herself up. We both returned to the meeting. That was the last I heard of this accomplishment.

This is not an unusual story. You and I have participated in it many times, in one role or another. Perhaps this incident turned out just the way she and I wanted it to, but I doubt it. I think that a part of her would have liked her success to be sung from the rooftops! She might have liked this group of friends to carry her around the room, to shake her hand, to hug her, to tell her what a wonderful businessperson she is. At home, she would have liked her husband and children to praise her for all that she has accomplished, with this contract being just the latest success. The family would say, the group would say, everybody would say, "Good for you! You worked hard for this! You are a wonderful person! We are proud to be a part of your life! We are happy for you!" Just maybe that is what she would have liked. Or maybe it is what I would like. Or you would like.

Here is a theory: Our fear of valleys moves us to smooth out the peaks of life experience. Celebrating the joys commits us to also acknowledge the depressions when they come along. We scan the horizon searching for bumps we can iron out and depressions we can fill in. When we share our joy with others through our need for recognition and celebration, we reveal our vulnerabilities. We open ourselves to their rejection as well as their love. Through participating with us in meaningful celebration, they also begin to know our vulnerabilities, so we are reluctant to let them in. We flatten and smooth our experience—at least that is what our public self shows the rest of the world. Our private self holds onto the peaks and the valleys. When friends, family, coworkers, and customers come along, we show them our smooth world. And our reflective self wonders about a better way.

 You have read far enough to have some notion of how this chapter on appreciation applies to you. Think back over the years; you probably have stories too. Think especially about what you have given: your hard work, your accomplishments, your attention, your caring, your giving. With that in mind, consider:

o How does each of your life roles look from the perspective of appreciation? Are some roles more rewarding in the recognition that comes from the role? Are some communities more appreciative?

○ What does your private self say to you about the recognition and gratitude you receive? What patterns exist in these comments?

○ What have you done through time to make sure that you are appreciated? What have you done to avoid appreciation?

○ Do you see certain people as responsible for the recognition you have and have not received? How would you describe them?

○ Think about a particular incident in which you did not get the appreciation you wanted. In an attempt to understand yourself better, run through this incident in your mind. Try to engage your more observant reflective self. Describe your behavior in at least two ways, once as you would typically describe it and a second time from an outsider's perspective. Write about this in your journal before continuing.

There are many possible reasons for missing out on appreciation besides our own avoidance of vulnerability. For example, it might happen because thoughtless people are not paying attention. These people may have come to mind while you were writing. But they are not here right now, and we are. Let's focus on the people we can do something about—if we choose. Our options are many and simple, when we are willing to be our more authentic and vulnerable selves.

Set internal goals, accomplish them, and recognize yourself. You probably set goals already, but you may not be using them to give yourself recognition. If you set an internal goal, work at it and accomplish it. That is reason enough to reward yourself. How can you go wrong in congratulating yourself on what you just did? You can't! You set the goal and you did it: recognize yourself. This is the most knowledgeable, sincere, and appreciative recognition you can receive, so don't miss out on it. It is appreciation from the person who loves you the most. What you get from others is icing on this personal cake.

Recognizing what you have accomplished can lead you to talking with others about it, if you want to. Success begets celebration. Talking about our accomplishments reveals their importance to us and we gather celebratory energies around us.

Concealing our need for recognition gives others nothing to celebrate. When your important life events come along, how will others know about them?

Celebrate others' joy. What is important in the lives of your friends, family, and fellow workers? Participate in their lives as you hope they would participate in yours. Show interest in their personal accomplishments. Seek out what is important to them. Appreciate them. Recognize a friend. Organize a party. Write a note. Praise small actions. Seed the world with small generosities. Carrying out these small kindnesses can be rewarding for you and has the additional advantage of supporting a celebratory culture that you may benefit from in other ways. And people will be more likely to want to celebrate your joy.

You are not the only person who has difficulty with appreciation. Many of us have patterns going back into our childhood that evoke responses to the recognition we receive. And don't receive. And are waiting for. Or are hiding from. We learned many important life lessons through the recognition and appreciation we got when we were children. Though we are grown, we are still those children. Find out about the child that others bring to moments of appreciation. Find out about your own child.

Cultural conditioning contributes. Many of us have been prepared by gender or race not to seek appreciation. For example, imagine a woman who has been conditioned to avoid seeking recognition and who is working in an office in which women seeking recognition are seen as too aggressive. The old conditioning plus the office culture both say no to speaking up for herself.

You may be a good giver but a poor receiver. Some of us are particularly good givers but not very good receivers. For various reasons, including professed doubts about our worthiness and our inability to control what others do for us, we show a pattern of giving to others what we claim we never wish to receive. We may imagine the recognition we would like—if only we could plan it and if only we could receive it without seeming immodest or self-centered.

Recognition fantasies are clues to what you want. Consider these three questions:

1. Do you regularly think about yourself, your accomplishments, and the lack of appreciation you receive for what you have done?

2. Do you regularly think about the kind of recognition you would like to receive from others?

3. If you had affirmative responses to questions 1 or 2, were you uncomfortable with that fact? Answering yes to both of these questions is a clue to your recognition needs.

Consider the possibility of telling others what you want. This is an alternative too many of us exclude. We learned long ago, at home or at church or at school, not to think about such things. Put that old learning aside for the moment and turn your mind to an upcoming important and positive occasion that could happen to you.

Planning for Praise

If you wanted it, how would you go about getting sincere appreciation for something that is important to you? Let's do some planning:

1. Start a new page in your journal with this heading: "What I Want to Be Appreciated For." Think about what belongs beneath this heading and write it down, whether you are getting recognition for it or not. This list is a good reminder of all you are doing. If it seems helpful, look back in your journal at your paths and roles and communities and world.

2. Comb through the list once, marking the items where you got appreciation. Look at them and remind yourself of what you liked and how it happened that you got it.

3. Comb through the list a second time, noting the times when you wanted appreciation and didn't get it. Do you see any patterns there? The journal entries you made earlier in this chapter might help.

4. Select one item from your list that is important to you and for which you could be appreciated within the next three months. Rewrite it as a heading at the top of a clean page.

5. Read the list titled "Getting Appreciation" that follows this exercise. Apply the list of appreciation ideas to the heading you just put at the top of the journal page. Create possible actions. Whenever you come up with a possibility, write it down under the label. During this listing, it helps to remember that you want appreciation and to forget modesty.

6. When you finish, you should have a list of possible actions for getting appreciation.

7. Select something from your list and act on it! Put it into action. Do something you have not done before. If you don't, you will continue to get the same level of appreciation you received in the past. You can change this if you wish. Others cannot change without knowing what you want.

Getting Appreciation

★ In the past, you waited around for appreciation and that did not work very well. This time, speak up ahead of time. Proclaim the recognition you want weeks ahead of time and tell people it is important to you. Yes, this is not subtle. You can even tell others what you want from them. For example, when Harriet left her last employer after fifteen years of loyal and capable service, she announced that she wanted a party and that she would dearly love to receive a kayak from her appreciative friends and co-workers. It worked! It is a lovely kayak! And so much nicer and more appropriate than what she would have received if she hadn't spoken up. Just because people were not spontaneous does not mean that they were not sincere. Telling them is much preferred to suffering because nobody knew what you wanted or that you cared.

★ Consider the possibility that you are not asking for appreciation because you think you do not deserve it. If that idea sounds ridiculous to you, then speak up for what you want.

★ Anticipate your successful completion of an event or project or behavior and tell people now that you want them to join you in two months to celebrate that completion. Ken quit drinking and told his four best friends that he wanted to take them to dinner in six months to celebrate his sobriety.

✻ When you reach a milestone at work that you would like appreciation for, invite others out for a beer to celebrate your milestone. No, don't invite Ken.

✻ Bring donuts or cake to the office to call attention to something you are doing.

✻ Tell friends about a new skill you have gained. Brag a little about the accomplishment and encourage them to give you a pat on the back by giving yourself a pat on the back.

✻ When you feel good about something you have done, or become, or realized, tell somebody who might understand. This might be especially helpful if you have a pattern of not talking about what you have done.

✻ Make appreciation less of an event and more a part of life. Honor in yourself and others the daily need for recognition, not just annual established rituals like birthdays.

✻ Become a person who appreciates others and what is important in their lives, and who likes to recognize life's joys with friends. Create opportunities to celebrate their lives.

✻ Create friendships that are rooted in appreciation. Give friends the opportunity to know you more deeply. They will then know when you would like them to join you in celebrating your many birthdays, accomplishments, relationships, learnings, projects, and ideas. Opening yourself to friends is a major step toward getting the appreciation you want and deserve.

Here is a closing story: Enrique owns and runs a small health food store. He lives, breathes, and eats health food six days a week. And he loves it! What's more, he's healthy. You do not have to hang around his store long before you begin to understand why this works so well for him. His regular customers come back again and again to tell him the wonders his products are working in their lives. They thank him and they buy more! Enrique is fed by the appreciation of the community he serves. He represents something to them in his role as a provider of healthy food. Ask him and he will tell you that he has created a signature path for himself that he loves and that others love to have him perform. They are frequent and eloquent in their appreciation of him. And what they appreciate him for makes it less likely that he is going to sneak into the back room and eat junk food. Enrique has created what he wants and arranged it so that others appreciate him for it.

o What is your "health food store"?

o What do you want to be?

o How could you get others to expect this of you?

o How could you ensure that others would appreciate you for it?

CHAPTER NINETEEN

Sustaining Hope

HOPE IS ONE OF THE ESSENTIAL COMPONENTS of your signature path. Look at past experience to see how hope sustained you through dark and difficult times. This chapter is about creating hope and carrying it on your walk along your path. We will create hope in some parts of your life by finding it in others.

EXERCISE

Hopeful Metaphors

1. Think about the playful parts of your life, the enjoyable times you have repeated, yielding similar feelings and satisfaction on each occasion. It might be quiltmaking, fly fishing, painting, gardening, playing music. Select a play activity that has at least five of these elements:

○ You see it as play.

○ You have returned to it over the years.

139

○ You don't do it every day.

○ It requires action and movement that can be seen by you and others.

○ It takes time to do, involving preparation, doing it, and follow-up.

○ It is hard at times; it involve struggles and discouragement as well as satisfaction.

○ You can build skill and knowledge in the activity through time.

○ It can be enjoyed as a novice and as a master.

○ You are drawn to thinking about it even when you are not doing it.

○ It can be shared with other people; you can talk with others about it or engage with others in doing it.

When you have come up with the play activity, test it against each of the statements above; it should meet at least half of these criteria.

2. We will use this activity as an expression of the hopeful side of your life. We are going to look at this play activity and find elements in it that would be useful to have in the work parts of your life. For example, I like to backpack; it meets many of the criteria cited above. I will use backpacking as an example as I guide you through thinking about your activity. So whatever I do with backpacking, you do with your play activity. Read on and you will likely construct yet another way of seeing your life, one that might serve you when you need hope.

3. Now that you have selected a play activity, describe it. In a paragraph, tell yourself what this activity involves and why you are attracted to it. For example, here is my abbreviated response: "I am an occasional backpacker who makes one or two trips a year into the mountains with friends, hiking four days into a wonderful wilderness carrying fifty pounds for six miles, at two to three thousand feet. That is a typical trip. Wow! And whew! Every trip is beautiful—and more

difficult. The mountains are getting taller. A day on that steep trail and I see its importance to my life."

You see what I have done; do the same for your activity:

○ Identify yourself within this activity; take on the role. ("I am . . .")

○ Describe what you do and how often. ("One or two . . .")

○ Express your feelings about it. ("Wow!")

○ Finish by relating this activity to the rest of your life. (" . . its importance to my life.")

You do not need to refine this statement. Just make sure that you have noted its key elements and that you have imagined yourself doing it.

4. Next, select a role that you perform in the rest of your life, probably a work role, but maybe a family or community role. Select one that meets some of the criteria laid out earlier. For example, I choose consultant, my primary work role. Select a role and then write it up as you did with your more occasional attractive role. Try to follow a similar structure. For example, here is my consultant role written in a way that resembles my paragraph about my backpacker role: "I am an occasional consultant, taking twenty or so trips a year into corporate America with clients—three days into another wonderful change opportunity, lugging my attaché case and carry-on across two time zones. That is a typical trip. Wow! And whew! Every trip is interesting— and more difficult. This work is getting harder. Hours on airplanes give me time to think about this work's importance to my life."

5. Next, consider how your work activity is like your play activity and vice versa. In my case, how is consulting like backpacking and backpacking like consulting? Find what you enjoy in your first activity and search for similarities in your work activity. Indicate the similarities with underlining, circles, and explanations. For example, backpacking and consulting share long, hard trails with no apparent end in sight. They share the satisfaction of having done it. They

share the camaraderie of co-workers. What do your activities share? Write about it.

6. What sustains you in your play activity? How do you get through the hard times? What keeps you coming back? Why do you stay with this form of play, especially if it can be difficult at times? Boil that down to just a few words and phrases. This is what sustains you. For example, I keep returning to backpacking because it is so rewarding to reach those beautiful vistas and because of the sense of accomplishment that comes with hiking a steep trail and reaching a beautiful place with friends. It is worth the exhaustion, worth wondering whether I will make it this time. And I remind myself that despite my fears, I have made it every time—so far.

   Write about your play activity before moving on. This is what sustains you and makes it likely that you will return. This is where hope resides.

7. Apply what you wrote about play to your work activity. See how it fits and does not fit. Then write about how your work is like your play. Search for ways in which you are drawn to your work that fit with some aspects of your play. Reach for new ideas and stretch your thinking as you do. This is an exercise in creating new views of work, so step outside your boundaries.

8. Look back through all you have written during this exercise. Can you capture what you wrote in item 6 in a short, useful phrase? Can you write something that might help to sustain you in moments of struggle? "Just do it!" "One day at a time." "I think I can, I think I can." "Nothing ventured, nothing gained." The world is full of other people's hopeful expressions; what is yours? Create one or borrow one. "I've made it this far" works for me. What personal slogan expresses your hopeful stance toward life? These short, expressive reminders link us back to our deeper truths in uncomplicated ways. It is no accident that religions and sports teams and advertisers find short cheers or prayers or slogans useful; they know the value of this focused expression. Write one for yourself.

9. When you have done this, put your slogan in a few places where you will see it—on your mirror, by your telephone, in your kitchen, in your appointment book, on your locker, on the face of your watch, in your screen saver. Put it in a place where you will see it often. And notice what it does for you.

Our work and our play often have a great deal in common. Not always, but often. If we are doing work we like, this is more likely to be true. But whether we like our work or not, we have to find ways of getting through it. Most work is hard when it is done day after day, year after year. That is one of the reasons we get paid to work and we pay to play! My hope is that in tough times your journal notes will remind you of what sustains you.

CHAPTER TWENTY

Trust in Action

EARLIER CHAPTERS IN PART THREE spoke of paths and passion, of intentions and action, of clarity and hope. We move toward concluding this book with trust, that positive web that holds individuals, families, and organizations together through serenity and adversity.[1]

Trust Defined

Trust is better experienced than defined, so let's create an experience that relates to what we have been reading so far:

---

1. I am indebted for this chapter to Jack Gibb, his ideas, and his book, *Trust: A New View of Personal and Organizational Development* (Cardiff, Calif.: Omicron Press, 1978).

1. Write "Trust" at the top of a journal page.

2. Write down the name of someone you trust highly who also trusts you. How would you describe the nature of your relationship? Why do you trust this person? What makes the relationship unique? What feelings do you have about this trusting relationship? Write a few of the words and phrases that come to mind about this person.

3. Think of another person you also trust highly. Pick someone you also have a great relationship with who is quite different from the first person. Write down this person's name and under it answer the same questions: How would you describe the nature of your relationship? Why do you trust this person? What makes the relationship unique? What feelings do you have about this trusting relationship?

4. Now imagine yourself standing on your life path. Imagine that path surrounded by the kind of trust that exists between you and your two friends. Imagine how you would behave as you move down your path: what you would say, how you would interact with others, what you would actually do. Write down five actions you would expect to take that depend on the trust of others. Your thoughts and notes will provide a backdrop for what we will do next.

Our challenge and opportunity is to create a path through life where trusting behavior makes sense for us. We trust others and they trust us, and we all behave accordingly. In the end, trust (or mistrust) comes down to what we do together. The test of trust is taking action. Action with others provides the possibility of building trust; lack of action does not.

Here are some boundaries that help to define trusting territory:

○ Though trust is essential, it cannot be dictated; it must be developed. It often requires great patience and time. There are no efficient ways of growing it. Everyone knows it is valuable, but whether others can tolerate the time it takes, well, that is another matter.

○ Trust is about connection—to yourself, people around you, the world around you, the path you walk. Its opposite, suspicion, is about separation and fear.

○ Trust draws people and ideas and positive feelings toward you. Trust is a receptive and gathering force. Suspicion pushes all this away.

○ Trust is not easily created and is easily destroyed. Trust that has been years in the weaving can unravel in a moment. It is a most precious fabric.

○ Trust is built, or rebuilt, by working with others. It is built with thoughtful action.

○ Trust relies heavily on individual choices and actions. An organization cannot trust you; it hasn't the heart. Trust grows as individuals recognize that they have been acting in concert with others over time, and that they have come to value that mutual support. When organizations have or lack trust, it is because of what individuals have done to nurture, neglect, or negate it. We build it; we destroy it.

○ Trust is not primarily a skill to learn, or a contract to sign. We are born with a need to trust; we learn about it as dependent infants and children. Even the most embittered of us recognizes the value of trust. Our bitterness often comes from a trust broken in our early years.

○ When trust is broken, we often assign intent or motive to the person who we think broke the trust. Often there was no intent, just misunderstanding.

○ The power of trust can be compelling. It offers the freedom to act and to respond. Trust creates or finds energy in people that they did not know was there. When trust is lost, a negative energy is created and rebuilding trust seems to be an immense and impossible task. It sometimes is.

○ Trust requires choices and commitment that go beyond rationality. It is not rational, but neither is suspicion and fear. Since neither alternative is rational, my pattern is to choose trust! If I am going to do something that I can't support with reason, I'm betting on the payoffs that come from connecting through trust rather than choosing to isolate myself through fear.

○ Trust cannot be pinned down in one activity or one feeling or one person. It is made up of a perishable patchwork of ideas like the ones in this list. It must be attended to daily to keep it alive.

The fabric of retirement parties, soccer teams, school plays, and family reunions is woven from patterns of trust. This underlying weave is more important than all of the mechanisms we put in place to sustain unity. Structures, procedures, values, roles, rules, goals, missions, and norms can work, given trust. In trust's absence, they tend to calcify or collapse or fall in a tangle, immobilized by their own weight. Think about the things that you celebrate or denigrate in the organized groups you are part of. Trust is likely to be woven through the organizations that you are proud to be part of.

How might we build trust with others? By doing things with them, by being with them, by seeing what they do and how they do it and liking what we see. Each time we do something with someone else that works for both of us, our mutual trust deepens. Through these shared activities, we each put down small, intertwined roots. The more actions we take over time, the more roots we put down. Multiply us by four and now we've got a team of people with shared interests and shared actions and more intertwined roots. You can see where this is going.

Trust grows deeper when this shared deep-rootedness is strengthened with time and experience. To be trustworthy, you have to satisfy others that your behavior maintains or advances their interests. Too often, we expect trust to build more quickly than is possible, a kind of "trust at first sight." There are no trust potions that reliably cause people to bond quickly and deeply. We must work at it to grow and shape the trust between us. Authentic change that lasts depends on deep, established trust. The changes themselves do not take as long as the trust building that is necessary to sustain the change.

 Think about what makes people successful in their lives. Not just material success, but the life success and happiness that can be available to poets and plumbers, tillers and teachers, gardeners and guitarists, you and me. Consider what trust has to do with success in your own life and work. Put three or four responses in your journal before reading on.

Trust does not start out there with others, but inside with you, with alignment of your three selves. These three selves, public, private, and reflective, have relationships with each other. Recall the last time you discovered two parts of yourself at odds with each other, unable to agree. For example, you may have noticed that your public self often cannot conceal the nervousness of your private self, despite what it is told to do. Or you have realized that your public self simply cannot live up to what your private self expects. And, of course, your reflective self has its own version of what is going on. These internal conflicts are worth exploring in relation to your trust in yourself.

Imagine living with this guidance on your signature path:

- Trust in yourself expands your self-knowledge, self-awareness, self-confidence, self-revelation, and self-motivation.
- Trust in yourself expands your curiosity, creativity, exploration, and willingness to risk.
- Trust in yourself makes it more likely that you will trust others; you are more likely to behave as if they are trustworthy.
- Trust in yourself makes it more likely that others will meet your expectations, that they will act trustworthy and trust you. Why? Because they can see your trust in yourself and in them.
- All of this will reinforce your trust in yourself. The old self-fulfilling prophecy does its lovely work once again.

Imagine a list that is the opposite of the one above, made up of lack of trust in yourself, self-doubt, doubt of others, fear building, and a regressive spiral feeding on itself. Imagine that shadow hanging over and guiding your signature path.

Your Choice

1. Read the two preceding "Imagine . . ." paragraphs again. Become very clear on their differences.

EXERCISE 2. Which paragraph best guides your signature path? Which paragraph would you like to have lead you through your life and work?

3. Asking you to choose feels a little simplistic, but choose. Life is more complicated than that. Complicated and subtle and mysterious and consuming. But several times each day, we choose trust or fear, awareness or blindness, integration or separation, based on our profoundly simple underlying beliefs about ourselves and the world. We make these choices and live them out in the world.

4. Choose and live your choice.

CHAPTER TWENTY-ONE

What Are You Going to Do Now?

THIS BOOK WILL BE ENDING SOON. Your signature path is one of action going forward. No backing up and redoing it, no erasures. This is it; you are sitting on your path thinking about it, or you are moving down your path. What are you going to do now?

Calendar

1. Look back through the notes you wrote while reading this book—all of those notes in your journal, or along the margins, or on scratch paper. Take twenty minutes or so to remind yourself of what you wrote about, to see what emerged as important to you. Do all this with the question in mind, What am I going to do now?

2. While reviewing your notes, write down a few alternative answers to the question. Don't try to decide which one is the best; just write down alternative answers to the question, What am I going to do now?

3. After you have written some action alternatives worth considering, test each of them against these criteria:

   ○ It is different from what you have been doing.

   ○ If you do this, it will move you closer to what you want your life to be.

   ○ When you ask, "And why is this important to me?" you like the answer.

   ○ It requires using your reflective self.

   ○ Thinking about doing it makes you curious or excited about the result.

   ○ You want to do it.

   ○ It is especially important to you and not nearly as important to anyone else.

   ○ If you do it, what you do will be observable to you and others.

4. When you have been through your notes and listed some action alternatives, put the list aside for a moment. Get out your appointment calendar, whatever form it takes. Display the next three months and beside it put the list of alternatives you just developed.

5. Look at the list; look at the calendar. Look at the calendar; look at the list. Your task is to do something magical that causes them to overlap: at least one alternative must end up on the calendar. If the list and the calendar affect each other, you will have done something about defining your signature path. If they don't, you will keep doing what you have been doing.

   For example, Valerie is a writer. She loves to write fiction and never has time for it. Her work as a lab technician, a community volunteer, and a mother keeps her busy. Yet she thinks about writing almost every day, and she has told others for at least a year that she is going to start writing again soon. With the help of the above list, Valerie signed up for an evening writing course that meets weekly for six months. She put it on her calendar and arranged to trade out babysitting. The course hasn't even started yet, but she feels better already! She made the time for the classes and she will make the time for the writing homework that the course requires. When she considers the criteria listed above, she finds that she is doing pretty well.

From your list of possible actions, develop something for yourself that meets many of the action criteria and can be put on your calendar. After five minutes, read the next step.

6. Here are some points to help you:

   ❍ This will probably not be easy! You have spent a lot of time and energy filling out your calendar in ways that do not include actions that you now say you want to take. Notice how many of your appointments and commitments involve other people and what they want to do. This is important stuff, but if you have no room for what you want to do, where is your signature path going? Entirely down other people's paths, that's where!

   ❍ It is not enough to think about the world or your action alternative differently; you have to put action on the calendar. Otherwise, it will go away—you can bet on it! Think of it as an appointment with yourself. An appointment to write, like Valerie's, or an appointment to walk, or read, or be with your family, or garden, or play music, or complete a project that only you seem to care about. When it gets on the calendar, you are likely to do it or move it.

   ❍ For your commitment to the action to work, you will probably have to set aside a series of times, so that it will become a part of your regular life, rather than an isolated event. Setting every other Saturday afternoon aside to take photographs is much more likely to change your path than just setting aside next Saturday.

○ Doing what you want to do from the action alternative list may mean that you do not do something else that is less important to you or that is being asked of you by someone else. For many of us, this is the hard part: you may have to say no to someone or something else in order to say yes to yourself. And if you continue to define your own path, this will not be the last time.

○ Do it now! Get something on the calendar from your list of action alternatives. If you can't fit it into the next three months, reach out further, but do get something on the calendar. Maybe it is just a start toward what you really want, but a start is more than you have now.

7. Congratulate yourself when you write your action on the calendar. This action is an essential step forward. Take the action! Do not give away the calendared time you committed to. Do not cancel it when the time comes because you are under pressure. If you must change it, find a new time before you let go of the old time you reserved. If you cannot find a new time, then don't give up the original time. You will notice that when you tell others you are busy and cannot attend their meeting or help with their project, they usually adjust. You don't have to say that you are going to be painting; just say that you are busy and they will drop their request for that time. And try not to blame others when you give up your time. If they get the time, it is because you chose to give it up. Try not to blame yourself either; try to observe yourself, what you are choosing to do, and how that affects what you want.

As we have been discussing throughout this book, there is much going on that leads to the visible marks on your calendar: your feelings, thoughts, and reflections; competing pressures within yourself for your time; the pressures from others. After all that, it is the observable actions you take, the marks you make, that define your signature path.

CHAPTER TWENTY-TWO

Where Are We Going Together?

THROUGHOUT THIS BOOK we have been in a receptive and search-ing mode. We have reflected on our selves in our worlds and on our paths. Through looking at our communities and our many roles, we have pursued the meaning of it all. What is the grand design behind our individual pursuits? What larger cosmic order might all of this have? Why is this so important to us?[1]

We humans define ourselves in our reach for greater indi-vidual definition, our expression of uniqueness. We have a nat-ural drive toward finding ourselves. This drive exists whether we are aware of it or not. It is alive in our most and least human

---

1. This chapter is inspired by the works of Teilhard de Chardin, especially *The Phenomenon of Man* (New York: Harper Torchbooks, 1959).

actions. Whether we are embracing or killing, releasing or controlling, the drive toward our uniqueness is there. It is alive in schools, banks, office towers, ghettos, and convents and in prisons on both sides of the bars. In our most angelic and most demonic ways, in our most straightforward and most devious ways, we seek to define ourselves through what we do.

When we know ourselves better, we know more of what we bring to others. Our individuation makes possible our fuller participation in relationships and in communities. When we love ourselves, we can more readily love others, and when we hate ourselves, we can more readily hate others. All of this is included in the mysterious, necessary connection between our separate selves and our community selves, our alone selves and our social selves. We are never entirely apart from others nor entirely joined. We are both; our separateness spills over on our togetherness, which blends with our separateness, like the rolling and folding of dough by a baker. Now we are pressed into community with others. Now we struggle to find our unique selves. It is all happening at once, continuously.

As one human community, we are on the evolutionary edge of our psychic work together, though probably at elementary levels of expression. As individuals, we have a long way to go in our quest for finer expressions of ourselves. But the work we are doing individually is highly advanced compared to the work we have done in the full human community. We only get occasional glimpses of where we might be going together. Looking back at the patterns that birthed this emerging creation helps us to anticipate our evolving future. At least we imagine it does. And what might that evolving future be?

Much as salmon converge naturally and unconsciously on the streams that gave them first life, so we seem to be converging. We are not salmon, but we are salmonlike in our unconsciousness of how and why we are being drawn together. We too are drawn to the mouths of streams. Why are we all showing up? Why are we here, fin to fin, facing into this current of this stream at this time? Why have thousands of us converged on this stream? Why have you shown up? Do you know? Are you surprised at who is here? Are you surprised that so many were "invited"? Who is sending out the invitations? What is happening? Or has it happened? Or will it happen in the future? We all contribute our presence and our selves to an implied, unspoken promise of answers to these questions.

Around this planet, millions of us are gathering at the mouths of streams, streams of collective consciousness. We are drawn to these waters for purposes we did not intend, to learn what we cannot fathom. Drawn by a scent—by assent—by ascent. Our minds, bodies, and energies are aligned, facing upstream, awaiting the spring flood that will lift us up and forward together. Each of us is an individual bit of consciousness floating within the mass. Some of us are unaware that we are here or why we are here, staying busy, wandering around. Others of us believe that we know why we are here, what will happen, and when. Others continuously ask why they are here. And others are expectantly but patiently waiting.

We live in this biosphere, this fertile physical world that surrounds us. These are the waters we swim in. These waters hold the scent, the promise of something more for all of us facing into the current. And we are beginning to notice that we are connected to each other in thought, feeling, spirit, soul, intention, and awareness. We converge, creating patterns that we did not know we were here to create. Like salmon, we are drawn by the scent. We live, work, love, and wait at the mouth of this Stream of Streams. There is nothing more important to do.

Afterword

YOU JUST FINISHED READING a chapter that focused you on what you might do next and then a chapter imagining where we might be going together. These two chapters replicate what has happened in the whole book, now focusing and now imagining, on action and reflection, perspectives and intentions. By engaging you in nearly forty exercises or journal entries, I hoped to establish a pattern of awareness and reflection that would overflow onto your life outside of this book. By engaging you in thinking and writing often, I hoped to help your reflective self to become more influential in your life and work.

My role as guide has become clearer to me through writing this book. Much of my rewriting involved getting myself out of your way. With the help of manuscript readers and editors, I now understand better the differences between guiding, directing, leading, and partnering. As your guide, I have tried to help you consider your possible paths, rather than telling you what your signature path ought to be.

It is not that I am without prescriptions and advice. Here is a summary list:

○ Reflect, repeatedly and daily, on why you are doing what you are doing. Otherwise, you will forget and end up doing what you think others want.

○ You are creating your world by the way you see it; believe it.

○ Powerful learnings are hidden in your shadows; find them.

○ Use your life to define your work rather than using your work to define your life.

o You decide your signature path by walking it; everything else is preparation.

Keep reflecting; keep writing. Continue to stretch your mind and heart by engaging with people, ideas, and all that surrounds you. You have many other aspects of your life and path to explore. This book delved into a few but only alluded to others—family, spiritual life, play, and friendship come to mind. Perhaps that is what you will write about on your remaining blank journal pages.

The Author

GEOFFREY M. BELLMAN worked for fourteen years in major corporations before becoming an independent management consultant in Chicago in 1977. He has loved his work for most of these thirty-plus years.

His consulting focuses on creating and sustaining positive change in corporations. Areas he often explores with his clients include vision, values, mission, and strategy. His recent clients include companies in telecommunications, forest products, electric power, banking, and management consulting. This book developed from what he learned while working with clients who use work as a path to their life purpose.

Geoff has also written *Getting Things Done When You Are Not in Charge* (Berrett-Koehler, 1992; Simon & Schuster–Fireside, 1992), a book about succeeding in the midst of the chaos of big business. It has relevance to hourly workers and executives alike. He wrote *The Consultant's Calling* (Jossey-Bass, 1990) for people who want to know how external consulting can support a family and a life.

Geoff and his wife, Sheila Kelly, grew up in Washington State. They left in the mid 1960s to follow work and raise a family, in Denver, New Orleans, Tulsa, and Chicago. They moved to Seattle in 1981 and do not intend to move again. They have successfully emptied their home of children and are learning to be grandparents. They are both consultants and writers.

Geoff can be reached at: 1444 NW Woodbine Way, Seattle, WA 98177, 206-365-6220, or SigPath@aol.com.

Index

paths not taken, 117–118
public and private selves,
36–37
reaching for purpose and fulfillment, 16–19
reflective self, 40–47
roles, 86–87
shadow self, 50–51
sight building, 13–14
signature written in soil, 9–10
steep path, 120–122
suffering, 120–122
tabletop metaphor for world,
59–65
three selves, 32–37, 40–47
trust, 144–145, 149
Explanations of the world, 66–75
Eyes of friend exercise, 38

F
Fears
about depressions in life, 132
about passion, 115–117
"Finding Your Selves" exercise,
32–35
Four Sweet Views chart 46
"Four Sweet Views" exercise,
40–45
Frankl, Viktor, 124
Friendship
and appreciation, 137
looking into eyes of friend
exercise, 38
Fulfillment, reading for, 15–20
Future movement along path,
150–156

G
Gerund, life as, 57–58, 126–129
*Getting Things Done When You
Are Not in Charge* (Bellman),
159
Gibb, Jack, 144n

H
Headlines, looking behind, 68
"Hide and Seek" exercise,
117–118

Higher views of self, 39–47
Hold view of self, 44–47
Hope, 139–143
"Hopeful Metaphors" exercise,
139–143
"Hows and Whys" exercise,
16–19
Hows versus Whys, 16–20,
85–86

I
"Identity in Community" exer-
cise, 78
Individual-community dynamic,
78–81, 155
Individual-community grid,
79–81
Individuation, 154–155. *See also*
Self
Intentions, 125–129

J
Job. *See* Work
Journal writing
appreciation, 132–133,
137–138
four views of self, 45
passion at work, 114
paths not taken, 116
public and private selves,
37–38
reflective self, 36, 45
self-observing while performing, 30
suffering, 120, 124
three selves, 36, 37–38
trust, 148
work path, 100, 104–105
Joys, celebrations of, 132,
133–134, 136–137
Jung, Carl, 9

K
Kelly, Sheila, 76, 159

L
"Lighting the Shadows" exercise,
50–51
Love. *See also* Passion

reflective self, 31–38, 40–47,
125–126, 148
self-observing while perform-
ing, 29–30
trust and, 148
*Trust: A New View of Personal and
Organizational Development*
(Gibb), 144n
Trust, 144–149
"Trust Defined" exercise,
144–145
Trusting territory, 145–147

U
Understanding the world, 66–75

V
Vulnerability, avoidance of, 133

W
"Whys and Hows" exercise,
16–19
Whys versus Hows, 16–20,
85–86
Work. *See also* Paths
appreciation and, 130–138
boundaries around, 113
characteristics of, 100–102
compared with play, 141–143
destinations at, 24
dilemmas at, 73–75
exercises on, 135–136,
139–143
fulfillment in, 15–19
Hows and Whys of, 16–19,
85–86
intentions and choices,
125–129
journal writing on, 100,
104–105, 114, 116,
132–133, 137–138
learning of new skill at, 24
love and, 109–114

motives for working, 102–104
overworking, 113–114
passion and, 106–118
path of, 100–105
paths not taken, 115–118
questions on, 94
role for, 141–142
roles at, 84–85
and shadow side of passion,
115–117
structure in, 67–70
as substitute for love, 113–114
suffering and, 120–124
and tabletop metaphor, 61–63
three selves at meeting, 32–35
World
artificial ordering of, 66–70
author's advice on, 157–158
communities, 76–83
complexity of, 68–69
contents of, 59–65
cosmic order of, 154–156
definition of, 3
dilemmas of, 72–75
exercises on, 3–4, 60–64,
70–75, 78, 82–83, 86–87
as gerund or verbal noun,
57–58, 126–129
introduction to, 57–58
making sense of, 66–75
model of, 59–65
natural order of, 69–70
as noun, 57
roles played by individuals,
84–89
sea and sailboats as metaphor
for, 70–72
tabletop metaphor for, 59–65
Worlding, 57–58

Y
"Your Choice" exercise, 149

Berrett-Koehler Publishers

B ERRETT-KOEHLER is an independent publisher of books, periodicals, and other publications at the leading edge of new thinking and innovative practice on work, business, management, leadership, stewardship, career development, human resources, entrepreneurship, and global sustainability.

Since the company's founding in 1992, we have been committed to supporting the movement toward a more enlightened world of work by publishing books, periodicals, and other publications that help us to integrate our values with our work and work lives, and to create more humane and effective organizations.

We have chosen to focus on the areas of work, business, and organizations, because these are central elements in many people's lives today. Furthermore, the work world is going through tumultuous changes, from the decline of job security to the rise of new structures for organizing people and work. We believe that change is needed at all levels—individual, organizational, community, and global—and our publications address each of these levels.

We seek to create new lenses for understanding organizations, to legitimize topics that people care deeply about but that current business orthodoxy censors or considers secondary to bottom-line concerns, and to uncover new meaning, means, and ends for our work and work lives.

See next page for other books from Berrett-Koehler Publishers

Other leading-edge business books
from Berrett-Koehler Publishers

Getting Things Done
When You Are Not in Charge
Geoffrey M. Bellman

FINALLY, a book for all of us who are not in charge! Bellman offers practical guidance for managers, professionals, administrators, and supervisors on how to make a difference in their organizations and accomplish their own goals while supporting the work of others.

Hardcover, 298 pages, 9/92 • ISBN 1-881052-02-8 CIP **Item no. 52028-152 $27.95**

Repacking Your Bags
Lighten Your Load for the Rest of Your Life
Richard J. Leider and David A. Shapiro

LEARN HOW to climb out from under the many burdens you're carrying and find the fulfillment that's missing in your life. A simple yet elegant process teaches you to balance the demands of work, love, and place in order to create and live your own vision of success.

Paperback, 234 pages, 2/96 • ISBN 1-881052-87-7 CIP
Item no. 52877-152 $14.95
Hardcover, 1/95 • ISBN 1-881052-67-2 CIP • **Item no. 52672-152 $21.95**

Artful Work
Awakening Joy, Meaning, and Commitment in the Workplace
Dick Richards

DICK RICHARDS applies the assumptions of artists about work and life to the challenges facing people and organizations in today's rapidly changing world. He reminds us that all work can be artful, and that artfulness is the key to passion and commitment. Readers will learn to take an inspired approach to their work, renewing their experience of it as a creative, participative, and purposeful endeavor.

Hardcover, 144 pages, 3/95 • ISBN 1-881052-63-X CIP • **Item no. 5263X-152 $25.00**

Available at your favorite bookstore, or call 1-800-929-2929

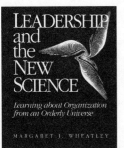

Leadership and the New Science
Learning about Organization from an Orderly Universe
Margaret J. Wheatley

"The Best Management Book of the Year!"
—*Industry Week* magazine survey by Tom Brown

OUR UNDERSTANDING of the universe is being radically altered by the "New Science"—the revolutionary discoveries in quantum physics, chaos theory, and evolutionary biology that are overturning the prevailing models of science. In this pioneering book, Wheatley shows how the new science provides powerful insights for changing how we design and lead organizations.

Paperback, 172 pages, 3/94 • ISBN 1-881052-44-3 CIP • **Item no. 52443-152 $15.95**
Hardcover, 9/92 • ISBN 1-881052-01-X CIP • **Item no. 5201X-152 $24.95**

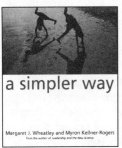

A Simpler Way
Margaret J. Wheatley and Myron Kellner-Rogers

A *SIMPLER WAY* is the widely awaited new book from Margaret J. Wheatley, author of the bestselling *Leadership and the New Science*. Here, Wheatley and coauthor Myron Kellner-Rogers explore the primary question, "How could we organize human endeavor if we developed different understandings of how life organizes itself?" They draw on the work of scientists, philosophers, poets, novelists, spiritual teachers, colleagues, audiences, and each other in search of new ways of understanding life and how organizing activities occur. *A Simpler Way* presents a profoundly different world view that changes how we live our lives and how we can create organizations that thrive.

Hardcover, 168 pages, 9/96 • ISBN 1-881052-95-8 • **Item no. 52958-152 $27.95**

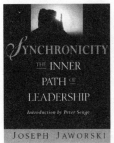

Synchronicity: The Inner Path of Leadership
Joseph Jaworski

S *YNCHRONICITY* is an inspirational guide to developing the most essential leadership capacity for our time: the ability to collectively shape our future. Joseph Jaworski tells the remarkable story of his journey to an understanding of the deep issues of leadership. It is a personal journey that encourages and enlightens all of us wrestling with the profound changes required in public and institutional leadership, and in our individual lives, for the 21st century.

Hardcover, 228 pages, 6/96 • ISBN 1-881052-94-X CIP • **Item no. 5294X-152 $24.95**

Available at your favorite bookstore, or call 1-800-929-2929

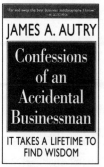

Confessions of an Accidental Businessman
It Takes a Lifetime to Find Wisdom

James A. Autry

IN *CONFESSIONS OF AN ACCIDENTAL BUSINESSMAN*, bestselling author James Autry blends candid and engaging autobiography with practical and realistic lessons in management and leadership. More than a memoir, it is a teaching tale for managers who seek to integrate their values in the creation of innovative, productive, and profitable organizations. Reflecting on his thirty-two years in business, Autry shares a lifetime of hard-earned wisdom about the art of business leadership, as well as the art of living a balanced life.

Hardcover, 250 pages, 10/96 • ISBN 1-57675-003 CIP • **Item no. 75003-152 $24.95**

A Higher Standard of Leadership
Lessons from the Life of Gandhi

Keshavan Nair

THIS IS THE FIRST BOOK to apply lessons from Gandhi's life to the practical tasks faced by today's business and political leaders. Through illustrative examples from Gandhi's life and writings, Keshavan Nair identifies commitments—to conscience, openness, service, values, and reduced personal attachments—and describes the courage and determination necessary to work and lead by them. He explores the process of making decisions, setting goals, and implementing actions in the spirit of service that is essential to the realization of a higher standard of leadership in our workplaces and communities.

Hardcover, 174 pages, 10/94 • ISBN 1-881052-58-3 CIP • **Item no. 52583-152 $24.95**

Reawakening the Spirit in Work
The Power of Dharmic Management

Jack Hawley

JACK HAWLEY responds directly to a widespread desire for spirituality at work, offering a practical vision of work permeated with "dharma"—deep integrity fusing spirit, character, human values, and decency. Through real-life examples, Hawley shows how people can create improved workplaces and more resilient, effective, and successful organizations.

Hardcover, 224 pages, 5/96 • ISBN 1-881052-22-2 CIP • **Item no. 52222-152 $24.95**

Available at your favorite bookstore, or call 1-800-929-2929